HE WALKED
THROUGH WALLS

Myriam Miedzian

Los Angeles July 12. 1968

My Dear Nadia,
I hope that this letter will find you in good health.
Dear Nadia, I miss you very much, when you left our house every room was empty a few days I went to see how you are playing and talking your language but I did not find you I was dreaming of you...

I hope that peace will be in this crazy world. All my life I have seen only wars: 1905 wen I was a child it was Rossia

2

Japanese war, 1911-1912 Balkan war, 1914-1918 world war one; 1919-1920 Polish Bolshewik (Rossia) war; 1938-1945 World war two; 1950-1952 Corean war, and now the Vietnam war, and a few smaller wars, I hope when you will grow up you would not have terible times like those your Pope went through and I wish you lots of happiness with great Love your Pope

Best regards to your Parents

Henyek Miedzianagora wrote this letter in 1968 to his three-month-old granddaughter, Nadia. The letter provided part of the inspiration for this book, a "memoir" written in Henyek's voice by his daughter Myriam Miedzian, Nadia's mother. Nadia, now a history professor, has written the introduction to the book.

HE WALKED
THROUGH WALLS

A Twentieth-Century
Tale of Survival

MYRIAM MIEDZIAN

WITH A HISTORICAL INTRODUCTION BY
Nadia Malinovich

Lantern Books • New York
A Division of Booklight Inc.

2009

LANTERN BOOKS
128 Second Place
Brooklyn, NY 11231
www.lanternbooks.com

Printed in the United States of America

LIBRARY OF CONGRESS CATALOGING-IN-PUBLICATION DATA

Miedzian, Myriam.
   He walked through walls : a twentieth-century tale of survival / Myriam
Miedzian ; with a historical introduction by Nadia Malinovich.
      p. cm.
   ISBN-13: 978-1-59056-149-2 (alk. paper)
   ISBN-10: 1-59056-149-X (alk. paper)
      1. Miedzianogora, Hersz, 1901–1995. 2. Jews–Poland–Biography.
3. Jews–Belgium–Biography. 4. Holocaust, Jewish (1939–1945)–
Belgium–Biography. 5. Jewish refugees–Biography.   I. Malinovich, Nadia.
II. Title.
DS134.72.M53A3 2009
940.53'18092–dc22
   [B]   2009024002

For Rosa, Avram, Dasha

With the hope that their lives will unfold in more peaceful times than those experienced by their great grandparents, Henyek and Betty Miedzianagora

Contents

Author's Note

The narrative of this book is based on stories my parents told over and over. My father's stories went back to his early years in Poland. In World War I, he, his father, and brother were accused of being German spies; they were imprisoned and sentenced to death. Thanks to my grandmother's extraordinary efforts they were pardoned the night before their scheduled execution. A few years later, when he was drafted into the army during the Russian–Polish War my father went AWOL. Both my mother and father told the stories of how they escaped Europe during the Holocaust. My father was the more frequent and more gifted storyteller, and whenever I think of them, I hear the stories in his voice. And so I have ended up telling them in his words, in the form of a "memoir." Because I did not ask enough questions when my parents were young enough to answer them, I have had to create many of the details. They are based on my knowledge of my parents' and other family members' personalities, as well as my historical research.

Historical Introduction

Nadia Malinovich

B Y WRITING THIS INTRODUCTION to my grandfather's "memoir," I hope to provide the reader with a historical context
in which to understand his poignant tale of twentieth-century
survival. His life was both extraordinary in many of its details
while at the same time exemplary of the incredible upheaval of
Jewish life in the twentieth century.

Like my mother, I took my grandfather's stories about
World War I and the Russian–Polish War, and especially my
grandparents' stories about their escape from Nazi-occupied
Europe, for granted. It wasn't until I started working on my
Ph.D. in modern Jewish history at the University of Michigan
in the early 1990s that I began to reflect critically on those stories, to think about how my own family history, as recollected
by my grandparents, fit with historians' accounts of those same
facts and events.

There are always divergences between oral and written history. Sometimes, it is the historical record that sets straight
stories that have been distorted as they pass down through the
generations. In other instances, delving further into apparent
divergences between "personal" and "official" history leads us
to uncover areas in which widely held assumptions about the
past have been distorted.

The assumption — common even in academic circles — that
Polish Jews could not own land prior to the creation of an
independent Poland in 1918 provides an intriguing example of
a gap between family history and the official historical record.

The fact that, prior to World War I, my great-grandfather owned large parcels of land and made a handsome living as a wood merchant was central to my grandfather's stories of his childhood and young adulthood. He and his brothers and sisters lived the life of landed gentry, with a variety of private tutors coming to instruct them in their country home. He described how he and his sister would ride on horseback around their estate, supervising the peasants who worked for them, and how his father's booming business took him on travels throughout the Russian empire.

It is only recently that historians have begun to debunk the popular myth that prior to the creation of the Israeli kibbutzim, Jews had no access to land and no familiarity with farming. In fact, tens of thousands of Jews were farmers in the nineteenth and early twentieth centuries. My great-great-grandfather was one of them. In his account of how his family acquired the land that led to their affluence, my grandfather refers to Tsar Alexander II's decision in the early 1860s to include Jews when he freed the serfs. According to family lore, it was this act that made it possible for my great-great-grandfather to purchase the land he was farming. In fact, Jews were never serfs and Alexander's decree was not directly linked to Jewish land ownership. However, some aspects of my grandfather's story mesh with historical reality. It was indeed around the time that the serfs were freed that — despite the persistence of an official ban on Jewish land ownership — some Jews were in fact able to purchase land.

The emancipation of the serfs went hand in hand with the development of a previously non-existent land market. Some particularly valued Jews were given outright ownership of land they were leasing from noble owners, while others managed to purchase land in their own right. Jewish landowners were obligated to take on Polish names, undoubtedly to legitimize their purchases and get around the official policy of banning Jewish land ownership. The family's very Polish surname, *Miedzianagora*, clearly suggests that it was a part of this group.

The freeing of the serfs was part of a larger liberalizing movement that included a lifting of a number of restrictions on Jewish occupations and settlements throughout the Russian empire. The 1850s and 1860s were a time in which Jews were moving into professions previously cut off to them and provisions were made for select groups to travel freely throughout the empire. It seems very likely that within these favorable economic and social circumstances, my great-grandfather was able to purchase the estate called Ronczyk and move beyond farming to become a successful wood merchant.

The story of my grandfather and his father and brother being accused of being German spies is one where family history meshes perfectly with recorded historical fact. During World War I, Jews were routinely accused of spying, and in some instances, executed for their alleged betrayal of the Polish nation. These accusations must be understood against the backdrop of the Polish nationalist movement, which was at its height during World War I, and had by that time become highly antisemitic. Poles knew that the outcome of the war would determine the future political status of their country, which had not been politically independent since the Polish-Lithuanian kingdom was partitioned between the Russian, Austrian, and Prussian empires in the late eighteenth century.

In this context, Jews were increasingly suspected of collaborating with Poland's enemies to keep the country from achieving its long-sought-after independence. Jews were alternately accused of spying for the Lithuanians, the Soviets, the Ukrainians, the Austrians, and the Germans, depending on who was occupying a particular area of the country. Given that the region of Kielce where the family lived was occupied by the Austrian and German armies in 1915, it makes sense that local Jews would have been accused of being German spies.

That a Polish nobleman with whom my great-grandfather had done business saved his life and that of his sons, is another example of family history meshing with the historical record, as the Polish nobility and the Polish-Jewish elite had had strong ties for centuries. It was the Polish nobility who first offered Jews very advantageous terms to settle in the Polish-Lithuanian kingdom beginning in the late thirteenth century in return for running the noblemen's estates. This relationship continued until the fall of the Tsarist empire. These close ties often exacerbated antisemitism in the general Polish population — in a highly stratified and impoverished society, resentment was often displaced onto the Jews, who had, through the centuries, been the visible face of the Polish nobility.

After Poland became an independent country in 1918, the country almost immediately found itself in a war — from which my grandfather went AWOL — with the Soviet Union. The borders of the newly independent Poland had been ill-defined by the Treaty of Versailles, and the Polish head of state, Józef Pilsudski, sought to expand Poland's borders as far east as possible. The end of this Polish–Russian War in March 1921 ushered in a time of relative peace for the Jews of Poland.

The country's first Prime Minister, the liberal Ignacy Paderewski (who remained in office for less than a year), signed a Minorities Treaty at Versailles that granted civil, religious, and political equality to all minorities including Jews. Many Jewish children started attending Polish schools and cultural adaptation to the Polish mainstream increased. While Poland continued to be a center of traditional Jewish learning, the general trend was toward a loosening of religious orthodoxy and an increase in secular enterprises. The inter-war years were the golden age of both Yiddish theater and Yiddish literature, and saw a major expansion of the Yiddish press. The Zionist and *Bundist* movements, started in the late nineteenth century, were extremely influential.

Although the Polish state was legally committed to treating Jews as equal citizens, antisemitism remained a strong feature of the new Polish republic. Jewish lawyers and doctors found themselves shut out from state hospitals and institutions, and civil service jobs of all kinds were generally inaccessible; Jewish business owners had difficulty getting state loans, and Jewish artisans had difficulty obtaining work licenses. Very few Jews were admitted to universities, and it was almost impossible for Jewish professors to obtain university positions.

Given this largely hostile political and social climate, coupled with a depressed economy, it is not surprising that many Polish Jews, including my grandfather, made their way to Western Europe in the 1920s. This emigration was on a much smaller scale than the earlier great exodus of Jews from Poland and elsewhere in Eastern Europe. In the late nineteenth century and before World War I, Jews from the Russian empire, propelled by both economic hardship and antisemitism, began leaving their homes in huge numbers. The majority of them made their way to the United States, whose Jewish population went from 260,000 in 1880 to over three million in 1915.

My grandfather's family belonged to a small stratum of Polish Jewry whose situation differed starkly from that of the majority who barely eked out a living, as tailors, watchmakers, hatters, leatherworkers, and petty tradesmen. His memories of the great shame associated with leaving for America capture well the prejudices of this Polish-Jewish upper class. Recent historical scholarship has tempered the popular notion, conveyed by my grandfather, that it was the most impoverished or otherwise desperate Jews who made their way to the New World. In fact, it was more often than not skilled workers, rather than those at the very bottom of the social ladder, who were able to amass enough money to undertake the journey to the port of exit and buy steamship tickets for the United States.

Certainly, however, the wealthy Jewish elite were much less likely to choose emigration than their less fortunate brethren, and this difference underscores the importance that economic motives had in pushing Jews from Eastern Europe. While anti-semitism certainly played its role, the predominant reason that Jews left their homes in Eastern Europe in massive numbers starting in the late nineteenth century was the same as that which propelled other immigrants — the promise of a better economic future for themselves and their children.

The great wave of Eastern European Jewish immigration to the United States was halted by the outbreak of World War I, and restrictive immigration legislation enacted in the early 1920s ensured that Western Europe became the primary recipient of Jews moving westward in the aftermath of World War I. For educated, French-speaking, relatively affluent Jews like my grandfather, immigration to France or Belgium was a particularly attractive option.

For the tiny country of Belgium, the arrival of these immi-grants completely transformed the Jewish community. Jews had been present on Belgian soil since the thirteenth century, but their numbers were negligible. In 1900, Belgian Jews num-bered fewer than 12,000. By the early 1930s, Belgium counted between 50,000 and 55,000 Jewish residents, a number that reached 70,000 by the eve of the German invasion. The major-ity of these immigrants, like my grandfather, hailed from the former Russian empire.

Patterns of Jewish social, cultural, and economic life in early twentieth-century Belgium were similar to those of France, the country that received the largest number of Eastern Euro-pean Jewish immigrants in the inter-war years. When Belgium became an independent country in 1831, the Belgian constitu-tion, following the French model, guaranteed political equality between Jews and other citizens. The inter-war years were marked by a great diversification of forms of Jewish social, cultural, and political life inspired in large part by the vibrancy of Jewish life in Eastern Europe. Jewish youth and sporting clubs, philanthropic organizations, and cultural and political associations flourished in Belgium, and over one hundred Jewish periodicals, including six daily Yiddish newspapers, were created between 1930 and 1940. It is no wonder that my grandfather adjusted easily to life in Brussels, and he would have continued to live there contentedly were it not for World War II.

While some of these new arrivals from Eastern Europe, especially those who settled in Antwerp, remained devoutly religious, the majority became secular; but secularization was not, for most, synonymous with assimilation. My grandparents' lifestyle and choices well illustrate this fact. After their marriage, they did not keep a kosher home, and observed only the major Jewish holidays. Their professional life brought them into regular contact with non-Jews, and they did not live in a Jewish neighborhood (ethnic/religious neighborhoods are much less prevalent in either France or Belgium than they are in the United States). And yet, my grandparents socialized almost exclusively with other Jews; their cultural references and world views were shaped first and foremost by the Jewish worlds in which they had grown up and continued to live in, in Brussels of the 1930s. They were also deeply sympathetic to the Zionist movement.

Belgium was good to my grandparents. So good, that, as my grandfather relates, he was able to send $10,000 to the First National City Bank in 1936, a decision that he attributes in part to his pessimism. While others (including my grandmother) thought that Hitler would soon fall from power, it was because he feared the worst that my grandfather made the decision to send a substantial sum of money to the safe haven of the United States. While this money did eventually help them obtain visas to come to the United States, the fact that it did not help them more quickly or more easily underscores the tragic fact that the United States took in so few Jews seeking to flee from Nazi-occupied Europe. As my grandparents found out when they reached Madrid in the summer of 1940, and made a determined effort to get visas to anywhere in the Western hemisphere, other countries were no better; in fact they were even worse.

My grandparents, mother, and uncle were part of a pitifully small cohort of European Jews — approximately 250,000 between 1933 and 1945 — who were able to find safe haven in the United States. Why did the United States not admit more Jews during this period, given the dire condition that the Jews found themselves in and the United States' historic reputation as a haven for the oppressed?

The immediate answer is the strict quota system that had been put in place in the aftermath of World War I. A growing nativist movement sought to restrict "undesirable" Southern and Eastern European immigrants to the United States, among them Jews. This lobby to protect the "Anglo-Saxon" character of the United States succeeded in getting Congress to pass legislation whereby only a limited number of immigrants from any particular country were to be admitted, with, unsurprisingly, very low quotas from countries like Poland.

President Roosevelt was not unsympathetic to the plight of Jewish refugees: he approved several projects for the resettlement of Jewish children in the United States in the 1930s, refused to expel 15,000 refugees who were in the United States on tourist visas in 1938, and did his best to make sure that quotas were made fully available to refugee immigration between 1938 and 1940. But even these small measures met with resistance from the State Department and Congress. The State Department was responsible for the day-to-day job of carrying out refugee policy, and the man in charge was Assistant Secretary Breckinridge Long who was both antisemitic and highly suspicious of foreigners who might be potential German or Russian spies. Today, the idea that European Jews of German origin could have been excluded from the United States as potential spies boggles the mind. Yet this idea played a role in American government refugee policy. Anne Frank's family could not obtain visas to come to the United States.

The fact that they still had relatives living in Germany was a disqualifier!

Another important reason that the United States did not do more to open the gates to Jewish refugees was, quite simply, that between rising antisemitism and a more general fear of immigrants taking away jobs, the American public strongly opposed modifying the quota system. A poll in March 1938, for example, found that only seventeen percent of the American population agreed with the idea of admitting "a larger number of Jewish exiles from Germany." A poll in early 1939 revealed that only twenty-six percent of the American populace approved of possible legislation for the entry of 10,000 German-Jewish refugee children! Any initiative to change the quota system would have had to come from Congress, and, given paltry popular support for these kinds of measures, it is not surprising that Congress was reluctant to do so.

Ironically, the more desperate the situation of European Jewry became, the more difficult it became for Jews to obtain entry visas: while 150,000 refugees entered the United States between 1938 and mid-1941, between December 1941 and May 1945 only 21,000 refugees were admitted into the country. My grandparents were fortunate in that they managed to obtain visas in the spring of 1941 when the quota system was still being respected. By 1942, the State Department began refusing to fill the already paltry quotas that existed for people trying to escape Axis-controlled countries.

The how and why of American refugee policy during the Holocaust has been a topic of both historical and popular debate for decades. Pioneering studies published in the late 1960s condemned the Roosevelt Administration for callously abandoning European Jews in their hour of need. Roosevelt, they argued, was unwilling to take the necessary political risk involved in pursuing the unpopular policy of saving European Jews. This criticism of the Roosevelt Administration tends to go hand in hand with criticism of American Jews' lack of activism. From this perspective, the majority of American Jews, caught up in their own agenda and worried about provoking antisemitism, did not have the courage to take on the struggle to save European Jewry.

More recent historians have tempered this condemnation of both the Roosevelt Administration and the American Jewish population, arguing that, given strong opposition to any change in refugee policy, the Roosevelt Administration had its hands tied. Rather than emphasizing the influence of antisemitism in American government policy, this school of thought contends that the powers that be simply did not care enough about Jews to make rescuing them a priority. Roosevelt and his administration did not grasp (or want to grasp) the enormity of what was befalling European Jewry, and, understandably, focused their energies on ensuring military victory over Germany and Japan.

The role that American Jews did (or did not) play in shaping American government policy has also been reconsidered in recent years. At the time, American Jews, for the most part immigrants and children of immigrants, were not remotely as secure of their status in American society as today's Jewish community. How could one expect them to take a forceful stance against United States government policy and organize into an effective lobby? Most historians now agree that even if American Jews had campaigned more aggressively for their European brethren, the chance that they could have pressured the government into changing its policy is somewhere between slight and nil.

At several points in the body of this book, my grandfather reflects on how impossible it was for him and his family to imagine what would happen, or was happening, to the Jews who had been deported. Is it surprising, he remarks, that his mother became paranoid after the war when she found out that her entire Polish family, including her children and grandchildren, had just been murdered?

The Holocaust is arguably the historical event that most boggles the contemporary human mind. Hatred of Jews, accused of being "Christ killers," had deep roots in Christian Europe. But at the time they and their Eastern European brethren were slated for mass extinction, Western European Jews, benefiting from the great reforms of the Enlightenment and French revolutionary era, were not an oppressed and despised underclass. They had become integral members of the European societies in which they were living, occupying a range of professions, political orientations, and social positions. To be sure, a new brand of antisemitism, which in distinction to traditional Christian anti-Judaism, posited the Jews as a dangerous "race" incarnating the evils of modernity, made substantial inroads into European society beginning in the late nineteenth century. And yet one would have had to have been a bit "paranoid" to imagine that this kind of hateful speech could actually translate into a master plot of mass murder.

Had the Americans surveyed in 1939 known that the Nazis would systematically gas and burn the Jewish children that they did not favor letting into the United States, would the percentage of people in favor of admitting them have been higher? Had President Roosevelt made it his business to find out what Hitler was planning in 1941, would he have exerted more pressure on the State Department to open America's doors to the refugees? Quite probably, yes. This is not to say that the hostility or indifference of so many Americans is not deplorable, or that the American government should not be faulted for its dismal record on rescuing European Jews, or that one should not criticize American Jews for not taking a stronger stance. At the same time, however, it is important to remember that the evil of the Holocaust was not something that those who lived through this period, whether Jews or non-Jews, were able to fathom the enormity of at the time.

What would have happened to my grandfather and his family had they not left Belgium in May 1940? Would they have been among the 26,000 Belgian Jews slaughtered in Nazi death camps? Perhaps they would have gone into hiding, leaving their fate to the goodwill of non-Jews who could have either protected or betrayed them. Perhaps my mother and uncle would have been placed by their parents in a convent, as were so many Jewish children during the war. Would their parents have survived and made it back to claim them? Would they have ended up as orphans in a Jewish children's home, or perhaps been converted to Catholicism by well-meaning nuns? Thankfully, we will never know. But it is certain that, statistically, my mother and her family were much more likely to be members of one of these groups, than that of the all-too-small cohort of European Jews who were able to walk through walls and make it out of the horror that was Europe, alive.

Sources for this introduction include:

Bartal, Israel. *The Jews of Eastern Europe, 1772–1881* (Philadelphia: University of Pennsylvania Press, 2005).

Dekel-Chen, Jonathan (Professor, Hebrew University of Jerusalem). December 2008. Telephone interview with Nadia Malinovich.

Feingold, Henry L. *The Jewish People in America, Volume V: A Time for Searching: Entering the Mainstream, 1920–1945* (Baltimore: Johns Hopkins University Press, 1992).

Hundert, Gershon, ed. *The Yivo Encyclopedia of Jews in Eastern Europe* (New Haven: Yale University Press, 2008).

Mendelsohn, Ezra. *The Jews of East Central Europe Between the World Wars* (Bloomington: Indiana University Press, 1983).

Schreiber, Jean-Philippe. "L'immigration juive en Belgique du Moyen Age à la Première Guerre Mondiale" in *Histoire des étrangers et de l'immigration en Belgique,* sous la direction d'Anne Morelli (Bruxelles: Ed. de l'Université de Bruxelles, 1996).

Wyman, David S. *The Abandonment of the Jews: America and the Holocaust, 1941–1945* (New York: Pantheon Books, 1984).

———. *Paper Walls: America and the Refugee Crisis, 1938–1941* (Amherst: University of Massachusetts Press, 1968).

Nadia Malinovich completed a Ph.D. in history at the University of Michigan and is the author of *French and Jewish: Culture and the Politics of Identity in Early Twentieth-Century France* (Oxford: Littman Library of Jewish Civilization, 2008). She currently teaches Jewish history at Sciences-Po in Paris.

Prologue

WHY I AM TELLING MY STORY

TODAY IS FEBRUARY 16, 1982. I am sitting at the Formica dinette table in my apartment on Gardner Street and looking out the window. It is a sliding window, almost the whole width of the wall. Our apartment is on the third floor and I am facing north, so if I look to the right I can even see the Hollywood sign. It is February, but in Los Angeles winter is on a permanent vacation. I look at the tops of the palm trees and the roofs of the stucco buildings, and on the other side of Sunset and Franklin boulevards, the Hollywood hills. This is what I look at, but what I see is something different. I see a farmhouse in Klucze, Poland. It is on a small island. The house and the woods all around are covered with snow. The river that makes a circle around the house is completely frozen. My brother Jakob, my sister Balche, and I are outside making snowballs and throwing them at each other and laughing. My sister Fella is sitting inside by the fireplace; she doesn't like to go out too much in cold weather. Maybe she is writing a poem.

One year ago, a few days after my eightieth birthday, I sat down at the same table, in the same weather, and looked at the same roofs, and palm trees, and Hollywood hills, and I made a list:

Jakob, my brother
Jagda, Jakob's wife
Josef, their little boy
Balche, my sister
Manek, Balche's husband
Dora, their little girl

25

Moshe, my brother
Ruchla, his wife
Laya, Malka, Samuel, Rifke, Chana, their five children...

I was just beginning to write down all the names, when I heard my wife Betty going clip-clop down the hallway that leads to the kitchen. She is always wearing slippers that are open in the back and have a platform, and make a lot of noise. Betty is only five feet and one inch tall, but she likes to look taller. She does not need the platforms or the high heels. She has such a personality everybody thinks she is much taller anyway.

Our kitchen is right behind the dinette with a counter in between. I didn't turn around when Betty came in, but I heard her put down a pot on the stove. "Dinner in twenty minutes," she announced.

First she didn't pay attention to what I was doing. But when she came over to get some water from the cooler next to the dinette — in Los Angeles the water from the faucet tastes the way smog looks — she saw that I was writing and she could tell I was not paying bills.

"What are you doing?" she asked. Betty always likes to know what everybody is doing. I didn't answer so she came and looked over my shoulder. Right away she understood. She gave a sigh you could hear all the way to Sunset Boulevard, and she tried to grab the paper away from me. I didn't let her.

"Why are you doing this?" she said. "It will get you even more depressed. Forty years have gone by. We got out; we are alive; we are very lucky — we have wonderful healthy children and grandchildren, a beautiful apartment. We are in good health for our age. You have to stop thinking all the time about what happened."

Betty is lucky; she doesn't think so much about what happened. She doesn't sit and cry like me. Maybe it is because she grew up in Germany and in Germany they teach the people from the time they are children not to show too much their feelings.

I didn't argue with her, but I told her to leave me alone and I continued with my list.

A few days later, when I finished it, the list was many pages long; it came to one hundred thirty-five people in my family murdered by the Nazis.

Betty is right when she says we have a nice life here in Los Angeles with the palm trees and the ocean and the sun smiling on you. Most of the time I am living a normal American life and not thinking about what happened. We go to Santa Monica and meet our friends and our cousins Frieda and Sammy. We bring folding chairs and sit on the grass on the promenade overlooking the ocean. We talk; we play continental rummy; we go for a walk on the promenade. Sometimes we go to Café Casino for a coffee, or for lunch. There you can sit outside and look out on the ocean — it feels like being in Europe.

Almost all our friends belong to the Belgian Jewish Society. Most of them have the same story like me — they were born in Poland and immigrated to Belgium in the 1920s. A few are like Betty and Frieda — they immigrated to Belgium from Germany. Some were hiding during the war; a few survived Auschwitz; and the lucky ones, like me and Betty, got out of Europe and spent the war years in the United States. Well, it was not just luck, but that is a long story and I will tell it later.

We started the Belgian Society about twenty years ago. We have dinners and parties and we raise money, mostly for Israel. One of the happiest days of my life was June 10, 1948, the day the United Nations voted to create the state of Israel. If only this had happened ten years earlier, Balche and Jakob and the others would still be alive.

I have been the treasurer of the Belgian Society for many years. I am very good with numbers. If I had been able to go to college I probably would have studied finance or statistics, or maybe accounting. But in Poland, I was not even able to finish high school — they took me out of school to fight in the Russian–Polish War. Even if I had finished high school, it would have been almost impossible to go to college. They had *numerus clausus* [restricted number] at the universities in Poland. This meant they only let a few Jews in.

I try not to think too much about what happened to my family, but for me it is hard. Sometimes when my granddaughters were little and I was having a lot of fun with them, maybe I was in Plummer Park in the playground pushing them on the swing, or maybe I was taking them to 31 Flavors for ice cream (they loved ice cream and so do I) I would look at them — so cute, so innocent, having so much fun — and I would think of Josef and Dora, and my other nieces and nephews in Poland, many of them about the same age when the Nazis shot them, and I would try very hard not to cry. A few times they caught me, "Why are you crying *pépé* [grandpa]?" they asked. "Don't be silly! I am not crying; I just got something in my eye."

This last year since I made the list, I am dreaming and thinking even more about Balche and Jakob and all the others and remembering our times together. Today I am starting to write down for my granddaughters — they are now twenty-six, thirteen, and nine years old — but even more for my great-grandchildren, and their children, and their children, the story of how I lived through and survived the wars that killed my family and darkened my life.

◆ ◆ ◆

I was only fourteen years old during World War I. Already I was in prison with my father and my brother Jakob condemned to death because they said we were spies for the Germans. When I was eighteen years old, it was the Russian–Polish War, and they took me in the Polish army to kill Russians. I ran away. When I was thirty-nine years old, World War II started and I had to run again. Since then, no one has tried to murder me. Betty and I got mugged a few years ago. A man followed us from the bank and knocked us both down to the ground in our garage, but he only wanted our money,

Henyek and Betty with granddaughter Debbie,
circa 1965

Henyek and Betty with granddaughters
Alisa and Nadia, circa 1975

not our lives. As soon as he got what he wanted he ran away, and we got up.

A few weeks ago, I went to get my hair cut. I don't have so much left, but once in a while I need a little bit, a trim. I go to a barbershop that looks like in the old times. Outside they have a barber pole with the red, white, and blue stripes. Inside the chairs are leather with a foot pedal. The barber presses on it and makes the chair go up and down. On the walls are black and white pictures from the 1930s and 40s. It is always the same young man, Scott, who is taking care of me. Scott is about thirty-five years old and whenever I go there he is wearing cowboy boots. He likes to *schmooze* and so do I, so now he starts to tell me about a movie he saw on television the night before. "What a great World War I war movie. The air war scenes with those biplanes were something else...."

"I remember that war very well," I say to him. "I was in prison with my father and brother. They were going to hang us."

Scott gets so excited when he hears this, he stops trimming the back of my neck. He is holding the scissors in his hand and looking at me in the mirror. "Are you kidding me?" he asks.

"Of course not," I tell him. "About things like this, I don't make jokes."

So then he starts to ask me a lot of questions. I tell him a little bit what happened.

"How cool is that!!" he says. "You were on death row in war time, and then at the last minute you got a reprieve. Wow! Just like in the movies."

"Believe me, being in prison and condemned to die, being in a war is not 'cool,' " I tell him.

A lot of Americans have trouble to tell the difference between movies and television and real life. They think that wars are produced by MGM or Fox Studios. You see a lot of people fighting and getting killed and when it is finished everybody, including the people who got killed, get up and go to the refrigerator and take out a nice snack and something to drink. At night they go to sleep in a clean bed.

I read in the newspaper not long ago that some young people think that in World War II the Americans were fighting the Russians; they have never heard of the Holocaust. I have to start right away to write down my story.

Part I

MY LIFE IN POLAND
World War I and the Russian–Polish War

1

W HEN I WAS A little boy, for a while, everything was good. We were never hungry or missing anything like so many Jews in Poland who were so poor. My father was a rich man. Because he was the only son, he inherited Ronczyk — this was a big farm and woods — from his father. He had four sisters, but in those times, always the son was given everything. So he became a wood merchant and after a while he sold Ronczyk and bought five other parcels of land covered with woods — all together he had 2,750 acres — and sold wood all over Europe from Russia to Spain. When I tell this to people, sometimes they don't believe me — "Jews were not allowed to own land in Poland or Russia," they tell me. "You must be mistaken." They are right that Jews were not allowed to own land, but what they don't know is that there were exceptions. My family was one of them. How did this happen?

My grandfather was a farmer. He rented land — Ronczyk — in Russian Poland. In 1861, when Tsar Alexander II gave an order that if somebody farms land, from this and this date it belongs to him — this is called in English the "freeing of the serfs" — he decided to include Jews. As a result, those few Jews who now owned land were permitted to travel and to do business all over Russia. This was a big privilege.

We lived in the province of Kielce on one of our properties, called Klucze. We were only about one hundred miles south from Warsaw, but by *drushke* [horse and buggy] this was a

35

big distance. So I was born and I grew up in the country on a farm. Before World War I, we grew much more food than we could eat. We had wheat, buckwheat, potatoes, turnips, beans, cucumbers, and a lot of other stuff. We had cows, chickens, ducks, geese. We even had a mill for grinding the wheat. Almost everything we ate came from our own land. What we and the farmers who were working the land for us didn't need we sold to the food stores or to the open market in Przedborz, the town near us.

The war changed everything for my family. There was a lot of fighting going on near us, so the armies started requisitioning food. They took whatever they wanted. What we needed was not their business and so a lot of times we were going hungry. My mother was hiding a few things in the cellar, but you could be shot for doing this, so she had to be very careful. But the food shortage was small trouble compared to what happened to us one evening in the spring of 1915.

It was a Friday night and we were sitting in the dining room finishing dinner. The table was set with a bright white tablecloth, and our best silverware and dishes that we used only for *Shabbos* [the Sabbath] and holidays. In the middle of the table were two big candlesticks with candlelight shining so bright. We were all dressed up. I especially remember the dresses that my mother and my sister Balche were wearing. In those days if you wanted a nice dress or suit, you had to buy fabric and go to a tailor or seamstress. Just before the war started, my mother had bought material for a new spring dress, but she made a mistake and she bought too much. So she decided to use the extra material to have the seamstress make for my sister Balche the exact same dress. Balche was only nine years old and she was so excited about this dress. All week, she was counting the days until *Shabbos,* so she could put it on. She was used to wearing short little girl dresses usually with a big bow in the back. Now she had a long dress just like *mamme*'s. It was a lilac color with little buttons in the front to the waist and a big white lace collar shaped like a "v" in the front and hanging over the top of the shoulders in the back.

We were all dressed up, but we were eating potatoes with fried onions, and bread. During the war, this is what we ate almost every day for lunch and dinner. Because it was *Shabbos* the bread was *challah* and we had a small *lekach* [pound cake] for dessert. My father was just pouring some homemade cherry brandy — my brother Jakob and I were old enough to get a little bit — when we heard from outside the sound of a *drushke*. We were living in the middle of the country, about ten kilometers from Przedborz, a small town where we had a lot of family and friends. By *drushke* this was far away; nobody dropped in to see us at night. We looked at each other — who could this be?

My mother looked worried. "I hope nothing bad has happened to Moshe and his family," she said. Moshe was my mother's son from her first marriage. He and his wife lived in Przedborz. My parents were both widowed when they got married to each other. My mother was still in her twenties and only had one son. My father was about thirty years older and already had seven children — some of my half brothers and sisters were about twenty-five years older than me.

Soon we heard a loud knocking on the door. *Tatte* [father] went to open it. Three soldiers carrying rifles marched in. I still remember I was surprised when I saw the rifles because I had read in the newspaper that the Russian army officers were very angry at the Americans because the rifles they had ordered had not yet been delivered. Very soon I wasn't wondering anymore how they got the rifles. I had other things to worry about.

One of the soldiers stepped out. He was wearing an army cap, but still I could see that his hair was red and curly. We didn't see very often people with red hair. He said, "We are looking for *pan* Josef Miedzianagora and his sons Jakob and Henyek."

"I am *pan* Josef Miedzianagora," my father told them, "and here are my two sons." By then everybody had gotten up from the table and was standing near the front door. Besides me, "everybody" was my parents, my brother Jakob who was sixteen — two years older than me — and my two younger sisters Balche and Fella who was only four.

Now the red-headed soldier told us, "Josef, Jakob, and Henyek Miedzianagora, you are accused of spying for our German enemies and we are here under orders to arrest you and take you to the prison in Kielce."

Those words put a knife through me. Only six months before, two Jews were accused of being spies for the Germans. They took them to the prison in Kielce, and a few days later they hanged them. I had heard that one of them had gotten into an argument with a rich Polish farmer, something about a horse. So when the Russian army was in our area, the farmer told them that the Jew was a spy.

"Officer, I understand you are following your orders, but someone has made a mistake," *tatte* said. "My sons and I would never...."

The soldier interrupted him. "I give you five minutes if you want to take something with you, and then we go. No discussion. We have here a warrant."

We couldn't believe how he was talking to our father. *Tatte* was such a respected man. When he walked down the street in Przedborz, people treated him like they treated the rabbi. Even the *goyim* [non-Jews] talked to him like to someone high up, someone special. We never thought that something like this could happen to him.

He tried again to say something, but again the soldier stopped him. Now Fella was grabbing *tatte* by the waist and screaming and crying. Fella was the baby in the family. When she was born, *tatte* was already in his seventies and she was his darling. When she was very little, *tatte* was carrying her around all the time; when she got bigger, he took her with him wherever he went. Later on, when he died, she was blind for three months!

You could look the whole world for two sisters more different than my sisters Fella and Balche, you wouldn't find any.
All her life Fella was afraid of everything. Balche was afraid of
nothing. Now she walked up to the soldiers; she put her hands
on her hips, and started to yell at them. "Why do you want
to hurt my father and my brothers? They are very nice; they
don't do bad things. Go away; go away from our house."

My mother ran over and grabbed her away. "Balche, be
quiet, you are only making things worse." Then she turned to
the soldier. "I'm sorry officer," she said. "She is only a child,
and you can see she is very upset."

"You Jews should learn how to discipline your children
instead of raising wild animals," he answered her.

I could have killed this *paskudniak* [disgusting person]
when he said this. The wild animals were not us Jews, but
them. A bunch of young Polish or Russian boys would get
drunk and start beating up any Jew they could find, or grab
Jewish girls and do with them whatever they wanted. When a
lot of them got together and did this, it was called a pogrom.
Jews were always afraid of pogroms. No Pole or Russian was
ever scared of a Jew doing anything like this to them because
Jews never did it.

But the whole time, I didn't open my mouth. And Jakob
didn't either. First of all, *tatte* was talking for us; second of
all, we were in shock; third of all, we were afraid they would
kill us right then if we said anything they didn't like. A few
Jews less in the world was no big deal to them. When Balche
started yelling at them, I was very scared that they would do
something to her.

Balche was what you call in English a tomboy except she
had more chutzpah than most of the boys. When we were
little she was always running around and playing games with
the boys, getting into trouble. One time, when she was maybe
seven or eight years old and our parents were not home, she
went into Jakob's and my room, took a pair of my pants, and
put them on. She rolled up the bottoms and then she came

outside where Jakob and I were playing and said, "Let's go out and play catch." We started to laugh when we saw her. In those days girls did not wear pants; we had never seen anything like this before.

"You are going to get into big trouble when *mamme* and *tatte* come home," we told her.

"Don't worry, I'll take them off before then," she said. "And anyway, I don't even care if *tatte* does get angry." All of us children were scared of *tatte*, not because he ever hit us — he didn't believe in hitting children and I don't either — but because he was such a big man, such a personality. The only one who was not scared was Balche.

So we went out into the woods and we were running around having a lot of fun. But when we got back to the house Stasha, the maid who was supposed to be watching us, saw Balche and started to scream at her, "How could you do such a thing? A girl dressing up like a boy; in my whole life, I have never seen such a thing. You come in and take those pants off and put on a dress like a girl is supposed to wear. Your parents will be so angry at me if they see you like this!" By then the pants were filled with mud because they were rolling down all the time, so Balche took them off before she came into the house. This got the maid even more upset because Balche was standing in her panties in front of her brothers. She grabbed her hand and took her into her room to wipe her off and put a dress on her. My parents never found out about it. We kept the secret.

Now Balche was alone in her room. My mother had taken her by the hand and told her to stay there and be quiet. I think that, after a while, even Balche understood that the soldiers had the rifles, not us, and it was better to shut up.

My father turned to my mother and said, "Cyna, I don't have a choice; we have to go with them." My mother tried to grab Fella away from him. It was hard because Fella was holding so tight to his leg. "*Gai, mein kind, gai mit die mamme*" [go, my child, go with your mother], *tatte* told her, and finally she let go a little and my mother got her away.

Mamme took Fella by the hand. "*Kim mit mir shepselle*" [come with me my little lamb], she said. "*Tatte* and your brothers have to go away for a few days and I have to pack a few things for them." And she took Fella with her into our bedrooms. The soldiers didn't want us to go into our rooms. Maybe they were afraid we would try to jump out the window and escape!

When *mamme* came back with a little bag for us, she looked at me and Jakob and *tatte,* and she said, "Don't worry. I will go tomorrow morning to the military commander, and they will free you." She was trying to sound like this was just a big mistake and she would take care of everything, but I could see she had tears in her eyes. She knew what had happened a few months before.

We wanted to hug everybody good-bye, but the soldiers pulled us away. They pushed us into the back of the *drushke* and took us to the prison in Kielce.

2

THE WHOLE NIGHT WE didn't close our eyes. The next morning, the guard took us out to see a high officer. He had a face like a pig — a nose so flat you could see into the holes. For lips, a thin opening at the bottom of his face. A chin he didn't have. There was maybe two inches between his eyes and the whole face was slanted back. His skin was pink and pock-marked and he had a twitch — all the time he was shaking his head to one side. Around his thick neck was one of those stiff, white collars with a little embroidery on it that the officers were wearing. His wide leather belt was lying closer to his chest than his waist. He told us that since we were German spies, they were going to execute us. "Don't worry, you still have a few days left," he said with a smile on his face. Probably he thought this was very funny. Killing a few Jews was for him the same as for me stepping on a few cockroaches.

My father tried to say something, but he cut him off, just like the soldier the night before. "We have witnesses," he said. "I don't have to listen to your lies."

We knew what was really going on. The year before, at the beginning of the war, the Russian army had advanced into most of Galicia — this was the part of Poland to the south and southwest of us that was under the control of the Austro-Hungarian Empire. Now in the spring of 1915, the Germans took back Galicia, and they were beginning to take over southern Poland. Later on, in August, they went all the way to

42

Warsaw and captured it. Whenever something bad happened, the Poles and Russians always blamed it on the Jews. If there was a drought, it was because the Jews put a curse on the farmers. If there was a big fire in Warsaw, it was because some Jew lit a match. If the workers were rising up, it was because socialist Jews were organizing them. But the reason working people were so poor was because Jews were dirty capitalists who were sucking blood from the poor Christian workers. Now they needed someone to blame for losing territory. So it was because Jewish spies — like us! — were giving information to the Germans. They always found people who were very happy to say anything the government or the army wanted to hear about Jews. Probably some Poles who were jealous of my father because he was a rich man told them that we were spies.

◆ ◆ ◆

When we got back to our dark cell — it was maybe nine feet by six feet with a tiny window so high up you couldn't get near it — *tatte* put his arms around us and said, "Children, don't worry, your mother is a very, very smart woman; you'll see, she will get us out of here." Whether he really believed this or was just trying to make Jakob and me feel a little bit better — we were both shivering — I don't know; but in the end, what he said turned out to be true.

We believed so much in what he told us that we started to feel a little less scared. Now he said, "Listen children, we are not going to sit here and think all the time that they could hang us in a few days. Until *mamme* has figured out how to get us free, let us keep our minds on other things. We'll tell stories; we'll talk about politics; we'll sing some songs."

And this is what we did. For the first few days, it helped. Underneath we were still shivering, but it helped.

The storytelling started right away because, as soon as *tatte* was finished, I asked, "Did that pig with the pockmarked face remind you of anybody?"

"Maybe you are thinking of the *gonif* [thief] who made *tatte* give him more *naden* [dowry] money than they agreed on?" Jakob replied. "He also had an ugly pockmarked face."

"That's right," I said.

"I haven't thought of that *gonif* in years," *tatte* said. "What he did got me so upset. Of all the more than forty young boys to whom I gave a *naden,* this was the only one who did such a thing. But it was small trouble. When you have big troubles like we have now, everything else becomes a speck of dirt."

In those days, a girl couldn't get married without a *naden* — at least she couldn't find a decent husband. Maybe she could marry a seventy-year-old man, or someone not very smart or a no-goodnik lazy fellow who couldn't hold a job. So my father gave *nadens* to a lot of poor girls so they could get good husbands. But this time he made a bad mistake.

"It was about four years ago, but I remember it like it happened yesterday," I said. "It was in the spring and Jakob and I were playing with a ball in front of our house. We saw a man coming on foot from the path that leads to the road to Przedborz. When he got close to us we saw the ugly pockmarks all over his face. 'Is *Rev* Yossl Miedzianagora home?' he asked. Right away I didn't like him."

"It was the way he talked. It wasn't nice," Jakob said, and he continued with the story. "We ran into the house and we saw you, *tatte*, sitting at your desk in your dark blue robe with an accounting book filled with numbers in front of you, and a pen in your hand. We told you that someone we never saw before came to see you. 'Take him to the dining room to sit down,' you told us. 'I have to finish writing down something, then I will come out,' and you dipped your pen in the inkwell and continued to write."

"How you boys remember such details!" *tatte* said. He was shaking his head in wonder. At that time, I couldn't understand what was the big deal about remembering details, but now almost seventy years later I am in my eighties and my memory is shrunk like a shirt you leave in the dryer too long and when you take it out it's maybe half the size it was before. Now I understand why my father was so impressed.

"All the time that you were talking to him, we were standing very quiet under the open window and listening," Jakob said. "We heard the man say, '*Rev* Yossl, I came here to tell you that I changed my mind about the match with Tova. Four hundred rubles for a *naden* is not enough; I want 500 and, if you don't give it to me, I won't go under the *chupah* [the wedding canopy].' You were so angry at him, you called him a *gonif* and a lot of other bad things, but in the end you agreed to give him the 500 rubles."

In those days, if two Jews shook hands on something, that was it. It was like going today to a lawyer and signing a contract. To go back on your word was a terrible thing. This *gonif* came two days before the wedding because he knew that it would be a terrible scandal for a poor girl to be left at the last minute, to be shamed, and that my father would give him the money, and he was right.

"I had no idea that you were listening to the conversation," *tatte* told us now. He had a smile on his face when he said this. The smile was interrupted by the sound of the prison guard opening the door to our cell. He was carrying a tray. On it were three pieces of dry bread and a glass of water. "I have a wonderful lunch here for you," he said. "But I don't know if it will taste as good to you as the *matzoh* you make with our Christian children's blood."

We each took a piece of bread and *tatte* put down the glass of water on the floor. The guard slammed the door and left.

"*Paskudniak, cholerny*...," we were cursing him as we were eating the bread. We were so hungry, in a few seconds it was gone, but our stomachs were still empty.

"How can they believe such a crazy story?" I asked.

"Whatever the priests tell them, they believe," *tatte* said. "If the priests tell them that we Jews kill Christian babies and use their blood to make *matzohs* for Passover, then this must be true."

"And if the priests tell them that we Jews killed Jesus Christ, and the Romans — who put him on the cross — had nothing to do with it, they believe that, too," Jakob said.

We were sitting very quiet now, with our heads buried in our hands. We didn't feel like telling any more stories.

After a while, we heard *tatte* singing in a very low voice, "*Koift zhe papirosen.*" This was a very beautiful, sad Yiddish song about a poor boy who is begging people to buy some cigarettes from him so he can have something to eat. Then he started to sing louder and louder. Jakob and I were both looking up now, and *tatte* put his hands up with the palms out to show us he wanted us to sing with him. We joined in and sang a lot of Yiddish and Polish songs.

So we sat in that cell with death looking down on us, and *tatte* trying to keep busy our minds with other things. After the singing, we told some more stories, talked about politics. But as the days went by, it got harder and harder to keep busy. After a while, we didn't have the strength to talk or to sing. Besides a few pieces of bread and water, sometimes we got soup that looked and tasted like dirty dishwater.

The night-time guard was a decent guy, not like the day-time *cholerny*, so sometimes he found a few extra pieces of bread to give us; but it was not enough. We were hungry all the time. We started to feel very weak, and tried to sleep just to make the time go by faster, but terrible dreams were waking us up. We were lying on the floor on some thin mats they gave us. It was cold in the cell, but at least it wasn't winter, or we would have been frozen. They took my father's watch away — it was one of those big round watches that was hanging on a chain from the vest — so we never knew what time it was.

They wouldn't let anybody in to see us, but on the second day they gave us a letter my mother brought — the envelope was already open. She wrote, "Don't worry. I am talking to the officers. I will get you out." First we had hope; we wanted to believe her. Also it was hard for me and Jakob to believe that they would kill such a respected man like our father.

By the third day, we were getting very scared. By the fourth day, we saw that our father's hair and the beard that covered his chest were no longer brown mixed with gray; overnight they had become the color of snow.

On the sixth day, the night-time guard came into the cell. First, he stood and looked at us with a face good for a funeral. Then he was rubbing his hand up and down on his chin. Finally he said, "I don't bring you good news." He didn't need to tell us anything more; we understood already. But he continued and told us that they were going to hang us in the morning.

We were hugging each other for a long time, and then I only remember that I wanted it to be finished already. If I have to die, let it happen fast. Already, I was feeling like I was dead.

3

ON THE MORNING OF the seventh day, the *paskudniak* guard came to open the door. But instead of taking us to hang, he told us, "You Jews are very lucky. Late last night, orders came to release you. I don't know why." He shrugged his shoulders and looked disappointed.

For a few seconds we stood like statues — maybe he is putting on an act. He wants to torture us a little more and next he will tell us he is joking and take us to die. But then he yelled at us, "Why do you stand like this? You like so much our prison, you want to stay a little longer?"

Then we understood it was true. When a baby is born it lets out a scream to say, "I am in the world; I am alive." Now Jakob and I also let out a scream — we were just born a second time. *Tatte* looked at us with smiling eyes; his beard was already wet with tears. "Let us get fast out of this hell," he said.

Outside *mamme* was waiting for us in our *drushke*. I took a look at her and I felt like I was in heaven. When she saw us she yelled out, "My children! My husband!" and she ran to us. "Now I can breathe again," she said.

We hugged and hugged and hugged, and we were all crying and laughing at the same time. If someone looked at us, he wouldn't even see *mamme* because we were so much taller and we surrounded her. Finally we let go, and *tatte* asked, "My dear, dear Cyna, how did you save us? Last night they said they would hang us this morning."

"Yes *mamme,* tell us! What did you do to save us?" Jakob and I asked.

"I will tell you, but first let us get in the *drushke.* Fella and Balche are at home waiting. Fella has not stopped crying since they took you. While we are riding home I will tell you everything."

We got into the *drushke,* but first we said good morning to Piotr who was in front driving. Piotr was kind of a handyman for the farm and the mill. Whenever something broke, he fixed it, and when we needed to go somewhere, he was the driver. "Good morning, *panowie* Miedzianagora, I am very happy to see you," he smiled at us.

When we were in the *drushke,* we could see that *mamme* was looking and looking at *tatte*'s snow white hair. "The boys told me it happened overnight," he said to her.

"What you went through...," she said, shaking her head from side to side. "But you are alive; nothing else matters, and now I will fatten you up." And she opened a bag she brought with bread and white cheese for us to eat. "I knew those *cholernyas* would starve you. Look at you! There is almost nothing left on your bones."

That bread with cheese was one of the best meals I ate in my whole life. And when I looked around me — it was spring time and there was no cover on the *drushke* — I was thinking I have never seen anything so beautiful. On each side of the road were birch and oak trees and in some places even cherry trees with pink flowers. Wild flowers were everywhere. From the time I was a child, I was used to seeing all this, but it never looked like this before — such colors, such smells, and on top of everything a blue sky without one cloud.

Now *mamme* told the story of how she saved our lives: "Yesterday morning, Piotr took me again to see the commanding officer who told me that they were going to hang you this morning. I started to feel faint, but I couldn't let myself faint. I had to do something. But what could I do? For five days, I was running to every high officer. Most of them wouldn't even talk to me and those who did told me they have orders from higher up and there is nothing they can do. I got in the *drushke* to go back home. I was pulling out my hair; I had to think of something. Then I remembered, Jossl, that you have been doing business for many years with a Count Ramofsky and always you talked about what a fine, decent man he was — and thank God you once told me where he lived. So when we got home, I put on a dress fine enough to go to the home of a count — I was afraid the servants would send me away the way I looked — and I asked Piotr to take me to the Ramofsky's palace. It took a few hours to get there, and when I saw that palace so big a few thousand people could live inside, I got scared to knock on the door. But what choice did I have? This was my last hope.

"I climbed down from the *drushke*, stood up very straight, and walked to the door and knocked. The door alone was as big as a room. The butler came to open and I told him, 'Would you please tell Count Ramofsky that the wife of *pan* Josef Miedzianagora is here and needs to speak to him on a very, very urgent matter?' He asked me to come in and sit down and wait in the entrance hall — it was about five times as big as our whole house and the ceiling about five times as high. A few minutes later, he came back and said, 'The count will meet with you in his library,' and he led me into a room where all the walls were covered with books. The count was sitting behind a very elegant carved desk. He was much younger than I imagined."

"I think he is about forty years old," *tatte* said.

"Such a nice-looking man," *mamme* continued. "So tall, a head full of blond hair, and such kind eyes. He got up from his desk and came to shake my hand. 'I hope nothing bad brings you here today,' he said.

" 'Something very bad, I am afraid, or I would not have come here and disturbed you,' and right away I told him. 'My husband and my sons Jakob and Henyek are going to be executed tomorrow morning on false charges that they are spying for the Germans. Some jealous people must have made up a story and gone to the army. I have tried for days to explain to the army officers, but they don't want to listen to me.' I begged him to help. I even got down on my knees.

" 'Please *Panye* Miedzianagora. Get up. There is no need,' he was shaking his head from side to side, and he came and helped me to stand up.

" 'I have known *pan* Miedzianagora for many years. I know that he would never do such a thing. I must tell you that you are very lucky. My wife and I are giving tonight a dinner party and one of our guests is an old friend who is an army general. I will talk to him, tell him how many years I have known your husband, what a fine man he is, that it is not possible that he and his sons are spies. We have a telephone and I will ask the general to call headquarters right away and tell them to stop this execution and let your husband and sons out of prison.'

"I thanked him a million times and I felt like I was dancing not walking when I left the palace. But then, after I was in the *drushke* for a while, I started to worry. 'What if the general feels sick and instead of coming he sends his valet with a note? What if he is on his way to the palace but gets into an accident and is injured or even killed? What if there is a military emergency and he gets called to Czestochowa?' All day I was worrying. All night I didn't close my eyes. After a while, I got out of bed looking for something to do. I polished silverware so shiny I could see my face in it. I sewed buttons, I sewed hems, I darned socks, I polished furniture. Only now when I saw you come out of the prison, then I knew; none of these things happened. The general came to dinner and the count kept his promise and you are alive."

We had not said one word while *mamme* was telling this story. Now *tatte* looked at Jakob and me. He was smiling and he said, "So, didn't I tell you right away? Your mother is a very, very smart woman; she'll figure out how to get us out." And he bent over and gave *mamme* such a big hug we thought he would never let her go. "Cyna, we owe you our lives," he said over and over, and then he looked at us — we were wiping the tears from our cheeks — and said, "Don't ever, ever forget that." And I have never forgotten it.

When we all stopped crying, *tatte* told us, "As soon as we have had a few good meals and slept a little, we are going to go and thank the count."

"Of course, of course," Jakob and I said right away. We, too, wanted to thank this man who saved us, but also we were excited to meet a count and see the inside of a palace.

As soon as we got close to our house, we saw Balche and Fella standing outside. We waved to them and they came running across the bridge to the *drushke*. We all got out and they were jumping up and down and screaming and hugging us so hard. *Tatte* picked up Fella and she looked at him with a smile as bright as the sun. Balche was dancing around and saying, "*Mamme* did it! *Mamme* did it."

Now *mamme* told Piotr to take the *drushke* and go to Przedborz and tell Moshe and his wife that we are alive and at home. Then we walked to the house together. After this time, Fella was sticking to *tatte* like she was attached with cement glue.

4

A FTER THREE OR FOUR days, Jakob and I started to feel stronger. *Tatte* at this time was in his middle seventies; it took him longer to come back to normal. So after maybe ten days, *tatte*, Jakob, and I got dressed up. We put on white shirts with stiff collars that went up a little around the neck, nice beige summer suits and ties, and shoes so shiny they were fit for the army.

We got in our *drushke* and went to thank Count Ramofsky.

When we got to the palace, the butler told us that the Count and the Countess were not home. They together with many of their friends were invited for a week of entertainment to the palace of another magnate. Jakob and I were very disappointed when we heard this.

Tatte left a note with the butler. He had written it in advance just in case the Count was not home. This is how it was in those days. Only a few people had telephones, so if you wanted to see someone you had to go to their house. If they were not home, you left a note or a card.

When we got back in the *drushke*, Jakob said, "This must be some rich magnate's palace that they went to if they can entertain so many guests for a whole week."

"Well, it's good for our Jewish musicians that they can afford such things. How would they make a living without the magnates?" *tatte* answered him.

The Polish magnates were hiring Jewish musicians to play for them when they had dances, dinners, picnics for their guests. Jews were known to be very good musicians, and this has not changed. Look at Leonard Bernstein, Isaac Stern, George Gershwin, Irving Berlin. This is just a few. The magnates owned so much land and were so rich, they didn't need to work. The richest ones lived in palaces with maybe forty, fifty rooms and about the same number of servants — butlers, maids, cooks, and stable boys, who took care of everything for them. It was no big deal to invite twenty-five, thirty people to their palace to stay for a few days or a few weeks. So when they and their guests were not riding their fancy horses — they had stables with about as many horses as they had rooms in their palaces — Jews were helping them to entertain their guests. Some of the palaces even had theaters inside and, besides the music, they had actors come and perform plays for them.

Jews also helped the magnates run their estates: not the ones where they lived, for this they liked to hire their own kind — Polish gentry — who often were doing a lousy job. The magnates owned not only the estates where they lived, but they owned land all over — often in the Ukraine. A lot of times, they hired Jews to be the managers of these estates far away. So instead of hating the owners who they never saw, the peasants and caretakers who worked for the magnates — and lived in one-room huts with mud floors and ate potatoes every night — hated the Jewish managers.

We were sitting in the *drushke* talking about these things and how everything was always blamed on Jews, when *tatte* said, "Ramofsky is one of them. The other magnates are his friends; he and his wife go to their homes, their children marry each other, but he is not an antisemite, he is a *mensch*. In every group, there are always some good people. One time, Ramofsky even told me, 'You Jews get blamed for what we magnates have done to Poland with our *liberum veto,* and all the different kings we have brought in.' "

Jakob and I were very surprised to hear that a magnate would say this and that he would say such a thing to a Jew. What Ramofsky was talking about is this: In Poland, the magnates wanted to keep all their power, so they didn't want a strong king. From the earliest times, instead of having a hereditary king or a queen like they have in England and other countries, and one strong, united country, they voted for a new king each time one died. A lot of times they would choose foreigners — some of them very stupid — who didn't care about Poland, to be king. This was bad enough, but then on top of this, they had a *Seym* [parliament] made up of the magnates who had the *liberum veto*. This was the craziest thing you can imagine. Any magnate could stand up and say "I oppose" whatever the *Seym* had decided and they had to throw out the whole thing. With a government like this and a terrible location — stuck between Russia and Germany — it was no wonder that Poland was a big mess and didn't even exist as a separate country for so long. We Jews had nothing to do with any of this, and Count Ramofsky understood this.

5

JEWS DIDN'T JUST PLAY music for magnates; music was a big part of our lives. Everybody in my family played an instrument — I played mandolin and violin. My brother Haskell was such a good violinist, people hired him to play at weddings and other special occasions. When she got older, Fella learned to play violin. She had a very sweet singing voice and knew all the words to the songs. In the winter, when it was too cold to go out, we would get together with all the brothers and sisters and cousins and friends and play music and sing and dance — waltzes, polkas, not this crazy disco and rock and roll like they dance now. Balche was such a good dancer and she never got tired. It could be midnight — for us in the country this was very late — and she still wanted to dance.

But we didn't spend all our time dancing. Every day except *Shabbos*, we had teachers who came to our house. We were learning Polish, French, Hebrew, Yiddish, mathematics, history, geography — everything you needed to know. Because we lived in the country, there was no school nearby to send us to, so the teachers came to us. Pretty soon after we got out of prison, Jakob and I went back to our lessons. We were all learning together — except Fella; she was only four years old. It was a little like what they call here a one-room schoolhouse. Sometimes Salke would come to our school too. Salke was my sister Nachele's daughter, so she was my niece, but she was about the same age as me. Her brother Henyek was a lot younger. This is what happens when you have brothers and sisters who are twenty-five years older than you. During the war years and for a few years after, Nachele and her two children were living with us in Klucze.

Everybody was feeling so sorry for them. But, sometimes, bad luck becomes good luck. Around the time that I was born, Nachele got married. After a while, her husband Eli got into some trouble in Poland — I think he owed money from gambling and couldn't pay back — so he ran away to America and for a while she didn't hear very much from him. Then, when the war started, she didn't hear from him at all. This is why she came to live with us in Klucze. Everybody was feeling so sorry for her. Later on, after the war, finally Eli sent for her and the children and they went to live in Brooklyn.

In those days, mostly the poor Jews, and sometimes those like Nachele's husband who got into trouble, went to America. People in Poland were looking down on them — they said that in America you couldn't be a real Jew. You had to work on *Shabbos* and soon you were eating food that was not kosher and other stuff like this. All those poor Jews and their children were living in Brooklyn, Long Island, Beverly Hills, when the Jews who stayed in Poland were being murdered by the Nazis.

It was very difficult years from 1915 to 1918, but after our time in prison, we didn't complain about eating potatoes and onions every day, or about any of the other hard times that the war brought on us. At least World War I didn't kill us like World War II, but it ruined us financially.

A few years before World War I, my father had sold four of his estates — Pilcziste, Czatkes, Kontes, and Dombrova (Dombrova became a small town which is called Miedziana Gora). He kept only Klucze where we lived. He took the money — in dollars it came to about $145,000 — and he lent it out for interest. He did this because he was already in his seventies and he wanted to retire. During the war, the government declared a moratorium — people didn't have to pay back what they owed. When the war ended the inflation was so bad, that for his $145,000 you could buy a pair of shoes, maybe two pairs of shoes!

I still can see my father sitting for days at the table in the dining room, shaking his head, buried in his hands, from side to side. We had lost everything. The whole house was quiet except Fella. She was about six years old at this time and she was trying all the time to make *tatte* feel better. She was climbing on his lap, combing his hair and his beard, kissing him, singing songs. I think she helped him.

Usually when we sat down to eat lunch or dinner, everybody was talking; it was very lively. But now we were all sitting so quiet. *Mamme* was all the time trying to get *tatte* to eat something. He had lost his appetite. Then one day, it was at lunch, *mamme* said to us children, "I want you to know I am blaming myself very much. I wanted *tatte* to stop working so hard, so I encouraged him a lot to sell our lands." When *tatte* heard this he got very angry. "Cyna, you are talking nonsense! I made the decision, not you. If I had not wanted to sell I would not have sold. Who do you think I am — Menashe Whatever You Say? I don't want you to ever say this again, or even think like this," and he made a fist and hit the table. After this time, we never heard her say this again.

Menashe was a man in his fifties who lived with his wife Manya in Przedborz. He was very, very quiet, and Manya was talking all the time. They were married maybe thirty years and Manya was making all the decisions. Whatever she wanted, he was always saying, "Whatever you say, Manya." People used to laugh and make jokes and call him "Menashe Whatever You Say." They were giving a lot of nicknames to people in those days. Sometimes they were not so nice. One man who was not so smart, they called, "Motel *Golem*" [Motel the Fool]. Another was Shmuel *Hoiker* [Shmuel the Hunchback].

After maybe a week, *tatte* called us all together. We sat down around the dining room table and he said, "Listen, children. It's a terrible thing that has happened to us. We have lost everything except Klucze. But let us be thankful that we are all alive, that *mamme* saved Jakob and Henyek and me from being killed. So we shouldn't sit and cry. But I want you to learn something from this. I want you to make me a promise that later on, if you ever have, you will never keep *schmattas* [rags, liquid funds]. If you have, put your money into land, into houses, but never *schmattas*. I don't want you to ever make the mistake that I made." So we all promised, and all my life I kept this promise. I have never bought a stock. I always put my money into real estate, and this is why I have what I have today.

6

IN 1918, AFTER 123 years of occupation by the Austro-Hungarian Empire, Prussia, and Russia, Poland finally became an independent country. This happened thanks to President Woodrow Wilson. Ignacy Paderewski, the famous Polish pianist and spokesman for an independent Poland, came to the United States and convinced Wilson to stand up for Polish independence after World War I. So what did Poland do when it finally got independence and Pilsudski became prime minister? (Paderewski was prime minister first, but he lasted not even a year.) It started a war against Russia!

At that time — the Russian–Polish War started in 1919 — my parents had sent me to a boarding school in Radomsk, a town about thirty kilometers from Klucze. Most of the boys at the *gymnasium* [high school] were Christians; just a few Jewish families that didn't have any high school near them, sent their sons. One day, we were sitting in the dining hall eating breakfast when the school principal came in with two army officers. Right away we stood up. (In those days, students had to show respect, not like now. When we walked by a teacher or the principal in the hallway, we bowed down our heads.) One of the officers walked with a limp — he probably got wounded in World War I, or maybe in the Russian–Japanese War, or the Balkan War. He was very tall, and thin like a toothpick, and he had one of those big mustaches that curl up.

The dining hall was a big rectangle with a platform on one of the long sides. The long wood tables where we were sitting were perpendicular to it. The principal and the officers went up on the platform. The principal told us, "You may sit down now," and then he introduced the officers. "They have something very important to tell you," he said.

The toothpick started talking. "You are educated young men, so I do not need to tell you that Lithuania, the Ukraine, Belarussia belong to Poland, not to Russia, and certainly not to those criminal Russian communists. With that great patriot prime minister Pilsudski leading us, with our courageous young men fighting for the fatherland, and with God's help, Poland will take back these occupied territories...." He was talking and talking. But after the first few words, I understood that they came to take us into the army. I felt like somebody emptied a big pail of ice water over my head. I started to shiver, but I folded my arms in front of me very tight and I stopped myself from shivering.

When he was finished talking — the other officer was just standing there; he never opened his mouth — the principal told us, "Now you may finish your breakfasts. I hope your soup is not too cold." For breakfast we always had a milk soup with dumplings, but this is not enough for young boys who have appetites like elephants. We had also bread with eggs, cheese, jam, sausages, ham. I never ate the ham or the sausages, but now, I lost completely my appetite; I couldn't eat anything. It was only a few years since I had been locked up in a prison waiting to be executed. Now I wanted to scream at them, "You are trying to kill me again in another one of your stupid wars." But I sat very quiet, not saying a word.

Some students got deferments, but a lot of boys over a certain age — it must have been seventeen or eighteen years — who were not cripples had to go kill Russians. They didn't give us a medical examination. Anyway, I was so healthy and so strong — once I was showing off to Jakob, I lifted our kitchen table with one hand — it wouldn't have helped me.

They just asked us to run around the schoolyard a few times. I was running very slow, but it didn't matter.

They gave us time to pack a few things and to write letters to our families, and then they put us in a covered wagon and took us to the caserne. Some of the boys were very excited; they couldn't wait to get guns in their hands and start shooting Russians — more than 100,000 were killed — and come home big heroes. Some of these boys probably got killed; about 25,000 Polish people died in that war. I don't know for sure because I never went back to the *gymnasium*.

But now they were laughing about no more school and they were singing patriotic songs — I was singing the loudest of all. All I needed was for them to start calling me an unpatriotic Jewish coward! Already a few of them asked me how come I was running so slow around the yard. I told them that I had hurt a muscle in gymnastics the day before and I had a terrible pain in my right leg when I was running. So they left me alone. Besides, they had somebody else to pick on. Jan Warshowski was in our wagon. He was not Jewish but he was a *pedal* [homosexual]. The boys were laughing at him and saying that the army made a big mistake to take a *pedal*. "Everybody knows that *pedals* don't fight; they are girls," and then they started to say stuff that I don't want to repeat here — disgusting stuff about what Jan would do for the Russians if they took him prisoner of war.

I had never even heard about *pedals* until I was in the *gymnasium*. One day, it was maybe six months before this time, we were sitting at our desks waiting for the mathematics teacher to come into the classroom, and I heard some boys who were sitting near me talking.

"Since we are in mathematics class, let's make a list of all the *pedals* in the gymnasium," one of them was saying.

"Good idea, then we will add it up and we will know how many *pedals* we have here. This is a good exercise in arithmetic."

"It's a good exercise for six-year-olds, but it's a terrific idea."

Then they all started to laugh and one of them said, "I would put Jan Warshowski at the top of the list. He walks just like a girl and when he is holding his tea cup at breakfast, he lifts his little finger."

"Just like a girl," the other boys all said in one voice. Then they were talking about some other boys and arguing whether they were *pedals* or not, whether they should put them on the list.

Finally I asked, "I hear you keep talking about *pedals*. It sounds like something funny, but what is a *pedal*?" This made them laugh so hard, it took them a few minutes to answer.

"Henyek, you grew up on a farm, how can you be so innocent and ignorant?" one of them finally said.

Then they explained it to me. I thought maybe they were joking, it sounded so crazy, but I didn't want them to laugh at me anymore, so I said, "I always thought there was something funny about Jan Warshowski." A few days later we had a vacation and we all went home. I could never ask my father about something like this and I was thinking my brother Jakob is only a few years older than me, so he probably doesn't know about such things either. So I waited until I was in Przedborz visiting with my brother Moshe and his wife. When his wife was in the kitchen, I told him what the boys had told me about *pedals*. "Is this true?" I asked him. He started to laugh, "It's true Henyek, it's true. In Yiddish, we call these people *'feiga-lach'* [little birds]. Remember Shmuel Krinsky's son who went to live in Warsaw — he's a *feigal*. They like to live in big cities because there they meet a lot of others like them. It's not normal, but some people just have bad luck and they are born like this."

Now more than sixty years later I live a few blocks from West Hollywood — this is the neighborhood where the *feiga-lach* live. When we are driving down Santa Monica Boulevard, we see them walking down the street holding hands, kissing each other. It still doesn't seem normal to me, but so many things that are going on now don't seem normal to me. I don't know anymore.

I was happy when we got to the barracks and got out of that truck. Jan Warshowski never said a bad word to me and I didn't like how they were making fun of him. Jan stayed in the army only one day; none of the boys wanted to sleep in the same barracks with him. The army realized they made a bad mistake and they sent him back to school. I never saw him again after this.

For a few weeks they gave us training — we were running for hours, climbing up ropes and fences, hiding in bushes and trees, shooting at targets. This was torture for me. Even though I grew up in the country on a farm, I never liked outdoor stuff. The game I enjoyed the most was chess, and later on continental rummy.

When the training was finished, they sent us to Western Ukraine. I was very lucky. They gave me a job helping the cook to make meals for the men in the caserne; I was chopping onions and peeling potatoes from morning to night but this was okay with me as long as I didn't have to go and kill people or get killed. After a few months, I even got a leave to go home for a few days — I still have a picture with me in my uniform and my brothers and sisters and cousins and friends all around me.

Soon after I got back from leave, an officer came into the barracks early one morning just as we were waking up. "I have some good news for you," he told us. "You will now have an opportunity to prove your courage, your manhood. I have orders here to send you to the front to fight the Russian enemy. You will be leaving by Friday at the latest. You will come home heroes. Your mothers, your girlfriends, your whole family will be proud of you."

When I heard this, right away, I decided to run. But how? I was thinking what to do while I was getting dressed, while I was eating breakfast, while I was peeling potatoes, while I was eating lunch. . . . All day I could think of nothing else. But I couldn't see how to get out. There were guards surrounding the barracks day and night. If they caught me trying to run away, they would shoot me. I could steal an officer's outfit and badge and get on a horse and ride out. But how could I steal an officer's outfit? If they caught me trying to do this, they would shoot me. Every idea I had finished with me getting shot. Better already to go to the front. At least I had a chance to stay alive. I couldn't sleep all night.

When I came into the kitchen the next morning, Czeslaw the cook was very upset and saying over and over, "*niech go szlag trafi* [damn him]." When he saw me, he said, "Because of that stupid boy, we are missing ten loaves of bread. What am I going to do? The soldiers will complain, then the officers will complain and they will blame me. They will say that I should have counted the loaves before the boy left them."

We were getting our bread from a town a few kilometers from the caserne. The baker was delivering it every morning. Now Czeslaw explained to me that the baker got sick during the night with the terrible flu that was killing a lot of people in those days, and so he put his son who was working with him in charge, and the son didn't bring enough bread. Very few stores had telephones in those days, so he couldn't call and ask them to deliver more bread.

As soon as I heard this, I started to feel better. I joined in cursing the stupid boy and saying how unfair it was that the officers would blame Czeslaw. I waited a little bit, and then I said, "Czeslaw, I would like very much to help you; I have an idea. When we were in training, we had to run so much, I have become very good at running long distances. If you want, I could run into town and back and bring you ten breads. It won't take very long and I will be back soon to help you in the kitchen."

"Henyek, this is a terrific idea," he said, and he gave me a big slap on the back.

"But what will you carry the bread in?"

"Don't worry," I said. "I have a very big knapsack, and if a few loaves don't fit in, I will take some rope with me and tie them together and carry them back that way." In those days stores didn't give you bags to put things in. You had to bring your own bag.

"You will need permission to leave the caserne," Czeslaw said. "I will go right now and talk to Jan Stankoski; he will help me." (Jan Stankoski was an officer in our caserne. He and Czeslaw were both from a small town called Zembrovi and Czeslaw's mother was the cook by Jan's family, so they knew each other from the time they were children.)

I went back to my empty barracks, got my knapsack, and put inside the civilian clothes I brought with me and what little money I had hidden. I went back to the kitchen and Czeslaw gave me a few pieces of rope. He already got a permission card from Jan Stankoski to show the guards. It was a big privilege for a soldier to be allowed out of the barracks. So I went to town — if you ran pretty fast you could make it in about a half-hour. Most of the time you were going through woods.

7

BEFORE I GOT INTO town, I went deeper into the woods and took off my uniform and put on my civilian clothes. I took a piece of rope out of my bag and tied my uniform up very tight, then I looked for a nice big heavy flat rock. When I found one, I tied it very tight around my clothes. A river went through the woods, so I took my package and threw it in the river.

When I got into town I went directly to the train station and found out what was the next train. "A train to Krakow is coming through in ten minutes," the clerk told me. As soon as I heard this, I relaxed a little bit. From the time I left the barracks, I could hear my heart beating so fast — my blood pressure was probably close to 200. And it was not from running — I knew if the army caught me, they would put me in front of a firing squad. That a train was leaving so soon was very good news. By the time they realized I ran away, I would be far from the barracks. I would have bought a ticket on the first train to go anywhere in Poland, but Krakow was one of the bigger cities. From there, it would be easy to get home. I could buy a ticket to Czestochowa, and then to Przedborz.

I was looking and looking for an empty compartment, but the train was crowded, so finally I went into a compartment where only one young girl was sitting. I said "hello" and I sat down. I didn't want to talk to anybody, but this girl was very friendly.

"My name is Teresa Koslowska," she told me right away, so I told her my name. Then she started asking me, "Where are you going? Where are you coming from? Are you a student?" In other times this would be normal conversation on a train, but now it made me very nervous. All the time we were talking I was worrying, How am I going to get across the frontier? What am I going to tell the guards? Will they hold me at the frontier? But I didn't let it show. I acted friendly. I told her I was a student and I had a vacation so I went to visit some cousins. She told me that she is from Krakow, but her father's family is from Western Ukraine, and she was visiting her grandmother who was very sick.

She was smiling a lot at me. I could see she liked me. I was a good-looking young boy and when *goyim* met me they never thought I was Jewish. They thought that Jews had dark curly hair and very long noses and couldn't speak Polish, or very little. My hair was brown, not very dark, and straight, and my nose was medium size. My Polish was perfect and even my name "Henyek" was one hundred percent Polish. My family name, *miedzian,* means copper in Polish and *gora* means mountain.

When we got to the frontier an officer came in and asked for our papers. He asked me, "What were you doing in Western Ukraine? How come a young boy like you is not in the army? You must have run away. Why did you run away?"

I told him, "I didn't run away. I am a student at the *gymnasium* in Radomsk, so I am free from the army. We are on vacation, so I went to visit my cousins." Now this girl Teresa was listening to all of this, and she was getting upset. After a while, she said to the guard, "Why are you making so much trouble for this young man? Can't you tell he is a student? He has a deferment. He is from a fine family; you should be more polite." She was a very good-looking blonde with high cheek bones, big blue eyes, and a nice smile, so he didn't get angry at her.

He said, "Don't worry *panna*, we are not looking to make any trouble, but I do have to ask *pan* Miedzianagora to come to the office with me. The train will be stopping here for at least a half-hour."

I followed him to the office. As soon as I saw the officer behind the desk, I knew I was in trouble. I could see from the way he said "hello" and from the look on his face that he was a *verbissine cholerny*. All the time that he was talking to me and looking at my papers, he was tapping the three middle fingers of his left hand on his desk. When I finished with my story, he said, "Why should I believe what you are telling me? You are the right age to be in the army; you are probably a deserter. I am going to keep you here until I have time to contact the military authorities."

I thought I was going to faint when I heard this. My heart was beating so fast and pounding so hard it felt like it was going to break open my chest. I could see he was the type who enjoys very much to have control over people and make them suffer.

I covered up how scared I was with a very loud strong voice. "My father has been on an important business trip to Krakow and he is meeting me at the station. He will be very worried if I am not on the train. Right away he will call the police, and his friends in the government. Could I ask you please to make a telephone call to my *gymnasium* in Radomsk, so you can find out that I am not lying; that I am a student there." This was taking a big chance. Maybe the school will tell him that they took me from the *gymnasium* to be in the army, and then I am finished. But what else could I do? A lot of people in Poland were against this war — the former prime minister Paderewski was so against it he went into exile — so maybe the school would protect me. Or maybe they would not want people to know that one of their students was shot for being a deserter.

"I am very busy right now; I don't have time to call Radomsk. You stay here and later on, in the afternoon, I will call the military authorities."

The officer who took me out of the train was in the office while this was going on. Now he leaned over on the *verbissine*'s desk and I could hear some of what he whispered, "Zbigeniew...important connections...who needs trouble? I can call." For a few seconds, the officer tapped his fingers even faster, and then he looked at me and said, "Officer Kitowicz has kindly offered to call your *gymnasium* in Radomsk." Then he started looking at some papers on his desk.

Officer Kitowicz went into another room where they had a telephone. He came back after a while, he bent over again on the desk, and whispered something. This time I couldn't figure out at all what they were saying, but when he was finished, the *verbissine* said, "You are free to go now. Hurry up or the train will leave without you."

I don't know what happened. Maybe someone at the school wanted to help, or because it was vacation time the person who answered the phone didn't have all the information and just told them that I was a student there. Maybe they couldn't reach anybody at the school — a lot of times in those days, the telephones were not working so good — so they decided to let me go. I think what Teresa said to the officer, and my letting them know that my father is a big shot businessman, helped.

When I got back on the train, I gave a big smile to Teresa and thanked her for talking so nicely about me. We made a little more conversation, then I told her that I was up drinking vodka with my cousins all night (this is what the *goyim* did), so I was very tired, and I needed to nap a little. It was true that I was up all night — worrying — so I was very tired, but much too nervous to sleep. I made-believe I was sleeping almost all the way to Krakow; this way she wouldn't be able to ask me any more questions. Before we got off the train, Teresa gave me her address and said I should come to see her if I am ever in Krakow. "I would like this very much," I told her. "It has been a great pleasure for me to spend this short time with you." We said good-bye, and I never saw her again.

When I got to Czestochowa, I had to wait until the next day to catch a train to Przedborz, so I walked over to my cousin Godol's apartment house and stayed overnight with him and his wife Esther. They were very happy to see me, but when I told them I ran away from the army, they got a little nervous. I think they were happy that I was staying only one night with them. The next morning, I took the train to Przedborz and went right away to my brother Moshe's house. I knew that he would be at his job in the town hall, but I was thinking I will go to his house and wait with his wife until he comes home and then he will take me in his *drushke* to Klucze. And this is exactly what happened.

When I got home, everybody was so excited and happy to see me. We were hugging and kissing, and hugging and kissing. I had already eaten at Moshe's house, but my mother brought out some *kapusniak* [boiled flanken with sauerkraut and potatoes] for me — this was one of my favorite dishes — so I ate again. In those days I could take a big pot of potatoes, turn it over on a plate, and eat all of it. Those days are finished. Now I am in my eighties and my stomach has shrunk, my brain has shrunk, my whole body has shrunk. I try not to think about this too much; it gets me depressed. I don't look much in the mirror either.

The whole family sat down around the dining-room table while I was eating and I told them what happened. We talked about what to do if they came for me. Fella started to cry. "I'm afraid they will come and put you in prison again," she said.

"Don't worry, we'll find a good hiding place for him — maybe in the woods," Balche told her.

"I don't think they will come to look for me," I said. "While I was working in the kitchen I was talking a lot with Czeslaw the cook. We became friends. One day — I think he was a little drunk — he said, 'A curse on Pilsudski and his war! My father was fighting in the Russian–Japanese War. He lost an arm and got a chest full of medals. A lot of good the medals did him when he had to find work to feed his family. When I was a child a lot of times, dinner was a piece of dry bread; my mother had to go work as a maid.'

"When I told Czeslaw that they were sending me to the front he said, '*Cholernya!* Why don't the generals go to the front and shoot each other!' It's true I got him into trouble because I didn't come back, but I was saving my life. Probably he told the officers that thieves must have seen me running to town, killed me for the money I was carrying, and left my body in the forest or threw it in the river. Anyway, the army doesn't have such good records — this is not a German bureaucracy — they'll forget about me." By the time I was finished with my little speech, I could see that my family was feeling better.

I was right; I didn't need the hiding places we figured out. The war didn't last too long — just long enough for about 125,000 boys to get killed — and the army forgot about me. So here I am eighty-one years old with two arms and two legs. One of the Jewish boys in Przedborz was not so lucky. A few months after I came back, the army sent him home. Both his legs were gone, and they made a collection in the synagogue to buy him a good wheelchair.

8

B Y THE TIME I ran away from the army, my father was already in his eighties, and so mostly Jakob was taking care of the farm and the mill, and Balche was helping him. Because they took me to the army, I never finished high school. But even if I had finished high school, I could not have gone to a university because of the small quotas for Jews. Some Jews went to the university in France or Belgium — in Poland everybody was studying French in school — and then came back to Poland.

I didn't have a profession, my family didn't have enough money for me to go into business, and I couldn't do any work with my hands. We were poor, but we still had our reputation. *"Es passt nicht ah Miedzianagora"* [it doesn't look right for a Miedzianagora], my father would say. (We were a little bit snobbish.) So I was helping Jakob and Balche to run Klucze, but there was not so much to do.

In those days we didn't have entertainment like now. Television didn't exist. In the country in Poland there was no radio and no movies. We had to make our own fun. The most fun was weddings. Here in America a wedding is five hours and that's it. In Poland a wedding was going on for days. We were playing music and dancing and singing and eating such good food. We saw so many friends and family. They came from Czestochowa, Lodz, Warsaw. It was as *freilach* [joyous] as the klezmer music we played.

It was not so much fun as dancing at weddings, but we had parties; we played chess; we played cards. Sometimes Jakob and Balche, and I were going to the Jewish *Kultur Verein* [Cultural Center] in Przedborz. Because we were living ten kilometers away, we couldn't go so often.

The *Verein* was started around the beginning of World War I by some of the more educated young people. They had a library with books that had nothing to do with Torah or Talmud — a lot of them in Polish — and they had a reading club. We were taking out a lot of books. Balche and I were reading, but not as much as Jakob. Wherever he went, Jakob always had a book under his arm. Even now I am reading newspapers and magazines all the time, but not so much books.

When we went to meetings, we were discussing politics a lot. Some members were *Bundists* (Jewish Socialists) some were *Revolutionists* (communists), and some were Zionists. Sometimes, I was thinking that the Zionists were right, that it was time for Jews to get out of Poland and try to go to Palestine and get back our land, Eretz Israel, but this seemed like a dream, something that would never happen. Mostly I agreed with the *Bundists.* In those days poor people were working in factories sixteen hours a day, some starting when they were six, seven years old. A lot of the factory owners treated their horses and their dogs better than their workers. The *Bundists* thought that Jewish people shouldn't study only Talmud, but that they should try to make life better for all workers — Jews and Christians. They wanted even poor Jews to learn to read Polish, but in the meantime, they were translating a lot of books about politics into Yiddish. In those days, poor Jewish boys went to *cheder* [religious school] at least for a few years and learned to read Hebrew so they could *daven* [pray], but this was the only education they got. So they could only read Yiddish and Hebrew.

The rabbi and a lot of people in town thought the *Kultur Verein* was a bad influence — against traditions and religion. They didn't like that the boys and girls were spending so much time together. So when the young people needed money very bad to keep open the *Verein,* and decided to put on a play, and charge people to see it, this was a terrible scandal — boys and girls acting in a play together, who ever heard of such a thing?!

Soon after they put on the play, a typhoid epidemic started and a lot of people died. The Przedborz rabbi said that the typhoid was a punishment for the young people's sinful behavior! And some people believed him. When people are very religious they believe whatever the rabbi — or the priest — tells them. It doesn't matter how stupid or crazy it is. If the rabbi had told them that the Tsar decided to become a Jew and called for a *mohel* [man who performs ritual circumcision] to circumcise him, they would have believed that, too.

In my family, we were not very religious. We kept kosher; Friday night my mother was lighting candles and we had a *Shabbos* dinner; on high holidays we went to *shul,* but that was it. Because we lived in the country we could get away with this. In Przedborz, all the Jews were religious, or they had to pretend they were religious. On Friday, the *shamas* [synagogue guardian] would come and knock on their doors to make sure the women were lighting *Shabbos* candles at the right time. Before Rosh Hashona, he would knock on doors to make sure the men got up for the prayers you're supposed to say before the high holidays. If someone didn't come to pray on Friday night and *Shabbos* — unless he was sick and close to death — the whole town was talking about him.

The Przedborz *shul* was something to look at. It was built in the seventeenth century. The outside was made of wood and looked very plain, like a barn. But inside was a vaulted ceiling — maybe forty or fifty feet high — carved with scenes from the bible. The pulpit and the wood beams were decorated with precious stones. From all over Poland people were coming to look at the beautiful *shul.* There was even a story — probably not true — that Napoleon on his way to kill Russians came through the town once and he was so impressed with the synagogue that he took some beautiful material with gold and silver embroideries off his horse's back and gave it to the rabbi, and one of the curtains in front of the Torah was made of this fabric.

The *shul* was on the river Pilica, and after the holiday services we young people had a lot of fun. With our friends we would go strolling back and forth on the bridge over the river, talking, making jokes, singing. We were all dressed in our best outfits. My brother and sisters and I loved to go to Przedborz and promenade on the bridge.

The summers were the best time in Klucze. It looked like the whole countryside was painted with every different shade of green that you could imagine. The air was sweet with flowers and pine and grass. When we were little, we ran around in the woods and played hide and seek and other games. Our parents always told us, "Never eat any of the mushrooms you see in the woods; they are poisoned and you could die from them." They called them "*michugana schwamen* [crazy mushrooms]." They said that many years before, a whole family from Przedborz went walking in the woods and picked mushrooms. When they got home, they cooked them for dinner and they all died. My whole life I never ate a mushroom.

When we were older we went for long walks in the woods with our friends and girlfriends. Sometimes we took a mandolin or a fiddle and we would stop and sit down and sing, or we were dancing. There were two sisters in Przedborz, Leah and Anya. They were our friends. Both were very beautiful. Anya had a small face with very delicate features and the biggest and darkest brown eyes I have ever seen. She is standing next to me and holding my arm in one of the few pictures from those times that were not burned by the Nazis. Holding my other arm is my sister Balche. She has high cheekbones and her straight hair is pulled back; she is also good-looking. Fella and Jakob and a lot of other family and friends are in this picture. It is after World War I, and already the girls cut their hair short. Anya's hair is very curly, a little bit wild.

The Przedborz Synagogue, built in the mid-eighteenth century

Henyek in uniform on leave with family and friends. Next to him on one side is his sister Balche, and on the other side is his friend Anya. His brother Jakob is standing on the extreme left. His sister Fella is in the forefront, on the ground.

Fella is wearing a short skirt, but Balche and Anya are still wearing long dresses — Balche's is a very light color, and Anya's is dark. I am in my Polish army uniform — it was taken during my leave — and I look very handsome. As I got older, I used to look often at that picture, wishing I would still look like that. It's hard to look in the mirror and see an old man with a wrinkled face and a neck with the skin hanging so loose it looks like it has nothing to do with the muscle under it. When it is not too hot, I am always wearing turtlenecks to hide my neck, but even then you can still see some of the skin hanging under the chin.

I had what they call a "crush" on Anya and she liked me very much, too. So sometimes we would go for a walk in the woods together and we kissed and we hugged, not much more — it was very innocent, not like now. Well, maybe some of the boys were doing more; they would brag about what they did, but I was never sure if they made up the stories or not. One cousin said he was having sex with a Polish woman who was married to one of the shop owners in Przedborz; another told us that he and his girlfriend were having sex in the woods. This was true because she got pregnant and he had to marry her. I was always very correct and I listened to my father when he said that the worst thing a boy could do was to get a girl pregnant.

About 75,000 Jews got out of Poland in the 1930s and went to Palestine before Hitler could kill them. Leah and Anya went. Many years later, when my wife Betty and I were in Israel, we visited them in Tel Aviv. They were such beauties but they didn't have luck. Anya's husband got run over by a car and died when he was in his fifties — there are a lot of crazy drivers in Israel. Leah's husband couldn't make a good living. He tried a few businesses but always he lost his money. I don't know why but not Anya and not Leah had children. And like me, they lost everyone in Poland.

It made me sad to see what happened to them. I looked at Anya — she was a middle-aged woman now, but the eyes were the same — and I was thinking, "What would my life have been if I had married her instead of Betty?" If my father had not sold four of our parcels of land, if we had not become poor, I would have probably married Anya and stayed in Poland. I couldn't marry her because I didn't have a good living. You didn't get married in those days if you couldn't make a living. Anya and Leah's parents were not poor, but they were not so rich that they could give me a big dowry and set me up in a business. If I had married Anya I would probably be living in Tel Aviv not Los Angeles. Maybe I would never have had children. Maybe I would have been a poor man. It's foolish to even think about this. One thing I am sure; Anya did not have a head for business like my wife Betty. With Betty I have had a first-class business partnership.

◆ ◆ ◆

Besides weddings, what I liked most of all was to go to Warsaw. Before they killed us, we were a very big family. Eleven sisters and brothers and so many nieces and nephews and cousins. Some of the older brothers and sisters were living in Warsaw, but they and their families came back a lot to Klucze to visit. In the warm months, almost all the time we had family staying with us.

Sometimes they invited us to visit them and their children in Warsaw. What a beautiful city! For me, going to Warsaw was like a small child going into a candy store. My sister Yochitl lived on the fifth floor and the building had an elevator! The first time I went — it was before World War I — I had never seen such a thing. I was riding up and down just for fun and looking at all the floors — the elevator, the cage, and the doors were all made of wrought iron so you could see through. Yochitl had a toilet that flushed — you pulled on a chain and water came out from a big tank on top of the toilet. She even had a bathtub with hot and cold water coming out of a faucet; I had never seen this before.

There were so many people in the streets. Trolley cars, cars, fancy *drushkes,* cafés. The Vistula River was lined with elegant mansions and ladies in long satin dresses with lace, wearing big hats with flowers and some even with little birds or fruit on the top. Later on after World War I, the women threw away those dresses and hats. They cut their hair and they were wearing short dresses without a waist and cloche hats, but still they looked very elegant. I was always a little bit scared when I first got to Warsaw. In Klucze, I was used to quiet, to looking at trees and fields. Przedborz had a few thousand people; that's all. But after a few days in Warsaw, I got used to being in a city and I was so happy to be there. I was walking around for hours with my nephews and nieces. Sometimes a few of their friends would come with us. We would stop in a café to have a cup of coffee or tea; or sometimes we would cross over the Vistula on the Poniatowski Bridge and go for long walks in Skaryszewski Park. Most of the time they were very nice to me, but once in a while they would start to make jokes about me being a country boy. They would say things like, "Henyek, you have learned very quickly to eat with a knife and fork; you are very talented." Or "It must have been difficult for you to have to put on shoes for the first time so that you could come to the big city." Always they would laugh and say, "We are just joking," but still it would get me upset. To this day, I get upset very easily when people insult me, or I think they are insulting me.

In Warsaw, a lot of educated Jews were assimilated. They spoke only Polish. If they went to a synagogue, it was a modern one where the rabbi was talking in Polish not Yiddish. If you went to some of the cafés, like the Café Lurs or Strassburger, they were filled with Jewish people all speaking Polish. Some of them were even marrying *goyim.* My family was not like this. A lot of the time we spoke Polish to each other, but we also spoke Yiddish, and in Warsaw we went to the Yiddish Theater. We were not religious, but we knew that we were Jews.

The beautiful Warsaw I knew doesn't exist anymore. In 1967, when Myriam came back from Poland, she told me "Warsaw was mostly very ugly — plain, drab, Soviet-style, cheap buildings that look like boxes with windows. The city was bombed to death during the war. They rebuilt one small part according to the old plans and that's very nice — you can see how beautiful it once was — except it looks like Disneyland with rows of supposedly very old houses that are obviously brand new. I guess as the houses weather, it will look more natural."

It takes so much work to put up all those houses, to build a city. I know. I built an apartment building in Brussels and then a few more in Los Angeles. Architects and builders draw plans; investors put in money; construction workers are sweating from morning to night laying the bricks or putting together the steel and the stucco. Electricians, painters, plumbers; so many people work to put together a building. And then in a few minutes the bombs destroy them. The same thing with people. The mothers carry the babies for nine months. When the baby is born, they are screaming and yelling from so much pain. Then the parents are waking up all the time at night, feeding the babies, changing diapers, washing them, holding them when they are crying, taking care when they are sick, working hard to pay for everything. And then in a few minutes, the bombs kill them.

9

ALL THOSE YEARS AFTER the wars, my father was feeling very bad about Balche. She was very smart and good-looking and she needed a husband who was also smart, and educated, and a *mensch*. Girls used to get married very early in those days. When their daughters were fifteen, sixteen, the parents already started talking to a *shatchen* [matchmaker] about a good *shidduch* [match]. Now my father did not have enough money to give Balche a good *naden* and this hurt him even more because when he was a wealthy man he had given so many *nadens* to poor girls.

One day, it was in 1926, all his worries came to an end.

Tatte went out in the morning for a ride on his horse. A few hours later, some farmers were banging on the door. My mother opened it. "*Panye* Miedzianagora, we bring you bad news. Your husband — we found him lying on the road and his horse was running with no one on it. He must have fallen off." My mother let out a scream that you could hear from miles away. My father was riding horses all his life; he didn't just fall off. She knew — he had a heart attack or a stroke.

He was about ninety years old when he died. Fella was fifteen and she was visiting one of our cousins in Przedborz when this happened. When *mamme* calmed down a little bit, she asked Jakob and me to go and tell Fella and bring her home. We got the *drushke* and the horses and started to ride. We didn't want Piotr with us, so we were sitting in the front;

Jakob was holding the reins. All the way to Przedborz, we didn't say a word. *Tatte* was very old, but we felt like he would never leave us — he was a giant; he filled up our house, our lives, our thinking, everything. Now there was nothing. When we got into town, Jakob said, "I'm scared; I wish it was somebody else telling her." I was thinking the same. "It's going to be something terrible," I told him.

First she wouldn't believe us. She was angry and screaming at us, "You are lying to me, you are lying to me! Why are you making up such a terrible story?" When she stopped saying that we were lying, she threw herself on the floor and was crying and screaming and crying and screaming. When she got up, she was blind. She stayed blind for about three months. In later years, I heard my children talking about this, they called it "hysterical blindness." Whatever it was, for three months she didn't want to look at a world without *tatte* . . .

Two of my older brothers and sisters were lucky — they died before Hitler — and a few were lucky because they moved away from Poland. My brother Shaya with his wife Franya and their four sons moved to Belgium in the 1920s. Their oldest son Herman was the same age as me! All the time, they were writing me letters, "Come to Belgium, we will send you papers. There is nothing for you in Klucze; here we will help you to get a good job in the shoe business." They were right; my mother, my brother and sisters and I were living in Klucze; we had enough to eat, but there was no future. (There was no future in another way, but who could imagine what would happen?) Jakob was the oldest brother and so he was taking care of the estate. Balche and I were helping, but it was not enough.

So finally in 1930, I wrote to Herman and his wife Emma and told them, "I am ready to come to Belgium." They sent me immigration papers and I moved to Brussels. This is why I am still alive.

Part II

MY LIFE IN BELGIUM

Ten Years of Peace in the Shadow of Hitler

10

I ARRIVED IN BRUSSELS with a few zlotys in my pocket and stayed with Herman, his wife Emma, and their two beautiful little children, Stella and Jojo. After my father died, everybody in the family who had a son was giving him the name "Yossl" in Yiddish, "Yosef" in Polish, and "Joseph" in French.

We all lived on top of Emma and Herman's shoe store on the rue de l'Escalier not far from the center of town. It was a good thing I had studied French in Poland, so pretty soon I was able to go to work as a salesman for a shoe company. I had never lived in a big city before, but right away I liked Brussels. It looked very different from Warsaw, but it was also very lively, with cafés, stores, trolleys, and lots of people on the streets.

Since her father Abraham was my first cousin, Betty and I met soon after I arrived in Brussels. Abraham's mother, Baile, was one of my father's four sisters and he grew up in Przedborz. When he was still a child, Abraham's parents died. A lot of people died very young in those days. Sometimes the women died when they were having a baby. When Baile got sick, my father took her to Warsaw to see the best doctors, but they couldn't help her. They didn't have the medicines like they have now; there were no antibiotics, and the surgery was not so good.

Abraham moved to Germany when he was a young man to try to make a good living, and there he married Bertha

Steinberger and they had two children, my future wife Betty and her brother, Julius.

Betty's parents invited me to dinner on a Friday night. They lived in an apartment on Avenue Clemenceau. The dining room was a nice size with a big mahogany buffet. On the top was a very fine piece of lace covering the whole length. The windows were covered with lace curtains, too. Betty's mother was a friendly, very dignified-looking lady, but a little stiff — she was a real *yekke* [German]. Her hair was about the same color as the lace. She was quite a bit overweight — today they would put her on a Weight Watcher's diet! She was not in good health and she was not a business woman. This is why Betty ran the business — a kosher butcher and delicatessen store — with her father.

Abraham was a very friendly person who liked to tell a joke and have a good laugh. Betty was twenty years old, not bad looking, but no beauty.

Betty had a big German Shepherd dog named Nero, and she was crazy about this dog. I got a little scared when I walked into the apartment and right away the dog ran over to me and started to bark. "Don't worry, Nero won't bite you," Betty told me and then she ordered the dog, *"Setze dich! Shtill sein!"* [Sit down! Be quiet!], and he obeyed her. "He only understands German," she told me. "He is very smart. Every day I say 'Nero! *Zeitung!*' [newspaper] and he runs out and gets *Le Soir* at the corner newspaper stand. The owner puts it in Nero's mouth and he brings it home. At the end of the week we pay for the papers." When she said "Nero! *Zeitung!*" the dog started to run to the door, and we were laughing. *"Nein* Nero," she told him. "You already got the *zeitung* today. I was just telling our guest how smart you are."

Julius was fifteen and he was a very handsome boy with dark curly hair, big brown eyes, and perfect teeth. But right away I saw that Betty was much smarter. Sometimes, later on, she would say, "If only I had been the younger child, I could have gone to the university and become a doctor. I would not

Betty with her parents and brother Julius, circa 1925

have had to leave school and run the store with my father when I was fourteen." By the time Julius was fourteen, the family was living already many years in Brussels and making a nice living. But Julius was not so good in school and university was not for him. Later on, he worked for us in our store — he was kind of a manager.

It bothered Betty very much that her parents didn't get braces for her teeth when she was young. She always complained, "Julius was my mother's favorite. If he had had buck teeth like me, she would have gotten him braces." Her mother made all the decisions about the children. Abraham respected her because she was so much more educated then he. Also, everybody thought that the mother knows what is the best for the children. I believed this, too. When Betty was in her fifties, she had her teeth pulled out and perfect straight teeth put in.

In the early 1920s, Betty's parents decided to move to Belgium for the same reason that I moved to Belgium — the terrible inflation after World War I. If not for that war they would never have left Germany. (If not for that war there would never have been a Hitler.) Bertha's family had been living in Germany for many centuries and, until the inflation, Abraham was making a nice living.

When he first came to Frankfurt, Abraham learned how to make frankfurters and *wurst* [salami]. Soon he became very good at it — he opened a kosher butcher and delicatessen store nearby, in Offenbach. He was twenty-seven years old when he married Bertha Steinberger. We have a nice engagement picture. He is a very good-looking, tall, thin fellow with a big, upturned mustache and a full head of brown hair, some of it falling on his forehead. He is wearing a suit with a long jacket almost to the knees, a vest underneath, and a shirt with a round, stiff collar. She is also very nice-looking — she has her hair in a pompadour and is wearing a white lace blouse with a high neck and a long dark skirt with a tight belt around her waist. She was still thin in those days.

Even though she was good-looking and smart, Bertha had a lot of trouble to find a husband. The problem was the dowry. Her parents owned a small grocery store in Frankfurt and made a nice living, but they had bad luck — five daughters. The father was a widower and the three oldest girls were from his first marriage. There was not enough money for good dowries, and the only men who would marry them without a dowry were *Ost Juden* [Eastern European Jews]. This they did not want. The German Jews looked down on the *Ost Juden*. They were poor, uneducated, they spoke Yiddish, and some of them — the Chassidim — even wore *payyes* [long curly side-burns] and long black coats and jackets with the fringes of their prayer shawls sticking out from under their jackets. The German Jews were more educated and wealthier, this is true, but still it was stupid. All over the world, people act stupid like this — for a long time, the light-skinned black Americans looked down at the darker ones. In India they still have people they call "untouchables" even though it is now against their law.

So what did the Steinbergers do with all those daughters? They sent the three oldest to Ida Grove, Iowa. The girls had an aunt who went to live there some time in the middle of the nineteenth century. She took them in and got them married to German–American Jews. In Iowa they didn't need a dowry. The parents preferred to send the girls to America and probably never see them again just so they would not have to marry *Ost Juden!* Maybe if it had been a mother, not a stepmother, they would not have done this.

It turned out that these girls were very lucky — when Hitler started killing the German Jews, they and their children were in America. They all made very good matches, and by 1908 one of the sisters came back to Germany with her family to visit. She even left her daughter in Frankfurt for a year to study. My future wife was born in 1909 and the American niece convinced the young couple to name the baby "Betty" — it was a stylish name in America in those days.

Bertha Steinberger was thirty-one years old and working as a sales girl in a confectionery store when her parents said "yes" to Abraham Goldberg. They liked that his family name did not sound Polish or Russian. They had already said "no" to another young man whose name ended in "ski." Also she was thirty-one years old. Today the young girls a lot of the time they don't even want to get married until they are thirty years old or more, but in those days it was very bad if a girl was not married by the time she was twenty-two, twenty-three years old. She was called an old maid and everybody felt sorry for her. If she had had a good dowry Bertha would have been married when she was nineteen or twenty.

After the wedding, the young couple lived in Offenbach near Frankfurt and this is where Betty was born. But when World War I started, some of the Christian neighbors got jealous because Abraham was not in the army — he could not be because he was not a German citizen — and he was making good money in his store, while their husbands were fighting for the *Vaterland*. So they complained to the city hall and they got him and his family sent away to Fulda, a small town where he opened another store. Betty had a nice life in this town. She was living there until she was thirteen years old. The only bad thing she told me about was, when she was a little girl, she invited a school friend to come to her house and play. The girl said she would ask her mother. The next day she tells Betty, "My mother said I am not allowed to play in the homes of Jewish girls." That girl and her parents were probably crazy about Hitler.

Betty was very smart in school and she was always reading books. From the time she was nine years old, she wanted to be a doctor. If there had been no World War I, she would have gone to medical school.

After the war, one of the rich American cousins wanted to bring the family to New York and help Abraham start a kosher-style delicatessen in Manhattan — instead of Carnegie Deli, it could have been Goldberg's Deli. But Betty didn't want to go to America. She had read a lot about all the gangsters in New York and Chicago. But more important, she belonged to *Blau-Weiss,* a Zionist youth organization, and she wanted some day to move to Palestine. Already at age thirteen, she had such a personality that she convinced her parents not to move to America. This was a very bad decision for her brother Julius. He would not have finished in a gas chamber in Auschwitz if they had moved to New York. Instead they moved to Brussels where they had family and this is how come I met her in 1930.

11

I WAS VERY IMPRESSED that first evening that Betty was running a business with her father. I was almost thirty years old and I had never had a real job in my life. In many ways, Betty and I were opposites. She was the oldest child in her family and her parents were depending on her from such a young age to help them make a living. I was the youngest boy in my family; I had so many older brothers and sisters, some of them more than twenty years older than me. I was the little brother.

Later on, after we were married, Betty told me that her father warned her even before we met that she should not get involved with me. "The Miedzianagoras were once very rich, and even after they lost their money they still could live off their farm," he told her. "Henyek has never had to work hard and he will never be able to make a good living."

She didn't listen to him, and after we got married he changed his mind very quick. We were married on April 29th, 1931. In our wedding picture, Betty's hair is cut in the short style that was *à la mode* in those days. She is sitting in her wedding gown, loose around the waist. I think this is called flapper style, with a veil made of tulle pulled very tight over the top of her forehead. I am standing next to her. I am already a little bit bald. We both look very stiff and serious — in those days the photographer told you to look like this on your wedding pictures.

Betty and Henyek's wedding portrait, April 1931

We would have gotten married even earlier. But while we were engaged, one day I came home from work — I was still living with Emma and Herman — and I found a letter on the night table in my room. I was getting a lot of letters from my family in Poland, and always Emma put down my mail on the night table. But this letter was not from Poland. It had a Belgian stamp on it and there was no return address. This was strange. I sat down on the bed and opened up the envelope, and started to read. It was an anonymous letter warning me that Betty was a loose woman with a bad reputation. I sat on the bed and read this letter over and over, maybe ten, twenty times. First I couldn't believe it. But then I thought, why would some-body write such a letter if it was not true? I started to think — Betty has such a strong will and personality; her parents listen to her and do what she tells them instead of the other way around. She doesn't care what people think. She even rides a bicycle around Brussels — in those days young girls did not do this. I had read that some communists and some artists — bohemians — were against marriage and believed in "free love." Now Betty wanted to get married — she was already twenty-one years old and it was time — but maybe when she was younger she believed this stuff and she had a history. If I married her everybody would be laughing at me.

I came out of my bedroom and showed the letter to Emma and Herman. Herman read it first. "I will tell you exactly what to do about this letter," he said. "Rip it up into small pieces and flush it down the toilet." And then he ran down the stairs because the bell was ringing; a customer had walked into the store. Now Emma read the letter. "Herman told you the right thing to do," she said. "Someone must be jealous or angry at Betty. I wonder who it could be. I will find out," and then she started to rip the letter, but I grabbed it from her.

I broke off our engagement. For many months we did not see each other. Everybody — not just Emma and Herman — was telling me that it was not true. How could I believe such a story? I started to think it over; maybe I was making a mistake.

And then one day, Emma came home from the bathhouse (in those days, most people didn't have a bathtub; you went once a week to take a bath) with a big smile on her face.

While she is taking off her coat she tells me, "I know who wrote the letter. I saw Bella Shmulovitz at the bathhouse. We were in the *schwitz* [the steam room] together and we started talking. From the beginning I was suspicious of her brother Ziggy because he proposed to Betty a few years ago and she said 'no.' And you know how Betty is, she acted like it was ridiculous for him to think that she might want to marry him. I told Bella how upset we were about what happened between you and Betty, and I exaggerated a little. I told her you were acting like someone who is in mourning, and Betty is crying all the time. 'It has ruined their lives,' I said."

She said this line like an actress would say it in a theater, very dramatic. I could see she was enjoying herself. (If Emma had been born in Los Angeles, she would have become an actress.)

She continued, "It worked! 'I can't hold it in anymore,' Bella told me. 'Ziggy wrote the letter. He didn't tell me, but one day, I said how sad it is what happened with Henyek and Betty, and he answered, "She just got what she deserved." When I heard this, I knew. After that it was not hard to get him to confess. He was kind of proud of what he did. I wanted to tell them right away, but he is my older brother and the way Betty acted when he asked her, it wasn't right. You shouldn't laugh in a man's face when he is asking you to marry him.'"

Forty years later, Betty was still upset that I believed the letter. Once she was sitting in the den in our apartment in Los Angeles reading a book about Sigmund Freud. When I came into the room she looks up and says, "Now I understand! You are kind of 'paranoid.'" She explained to me that this means to be always very suspicious of other people and fear for the worst. "First you believed that letter from Ziggy filled with lies, then just because your mother told you that Eduard came over a few times in the evening and we were staying up late, you started to accuse me of having an affair with him. I told you a million times, 'Eduard came over to talk business, to get advice'; he was thinking of opening a shoe store. I never even liked Eduard very much. I liked his brother Ignaz. I can guarantee you, if I would have had an affair it would have been with Ignaz. Even now, thirty years later, you are still bringing up Eduard from time to time. You still think that maybe I had an affair with him. You are really pretty paranoid," and she points to the book. She was very angry. Once around this time, she even told me that if I mention Eduard one more time, she is going to divorce me. I didn't really believe her, but I stopped talking about Eduard.

So I was wrong about the letter and I was probably wrong about Eduard — it's true that Betty was such a smart business woman, even men were sometimes coming to her for advice. This business with Eduard happened around 1948 when we were living again in Brussels. My mother was very sick and she was living with us. I had to go to the U.S. for a few months and when I came back, my mother told me about Eduard's visits and I got suspicious.

So maybe Betty is right and I am a little paranoid. Is this such a bad way to be? Anyway, what is "paranoid" in a world like ours? If I had not been so "paranoid" about Adolf Hitler, we would have been in Auschwitz in 1943, instead of on Central Park West. Starting in the early 1930s, I was listening on the radio to Hitler's speeches, and reading the newspapers. A lot of people including Betty were not so worried about Hitler. They laughed at him. He was such a *michugana* [crazy person], soon the German people would get rid of him. They were not paranoid enough.

After the war, when my mother came to live with us in Brussels, she was saying that there was a terrible noise coming from the ceiling and she was accusing us of putting in a factory upstairs to make this noise to drive her crazy. Nobody used the word "paranoid" in those days, but probably Sigmund Freud would have said that my mother was paranoid. But this is what I think: In 1939, my mother had five children and five step-children, about thirty grandchildren, and more than one hundred nieces, nephews, and cousins. In 1945, she found out that all of them — including the babies and little children — who were living nice quiet lives in Poland, not bothering anybody, were dragged out of their homes and either shot right away or gassed to death. So I ask you, what is paranoid and what is realistic?

12

B ESIDES EMMA AND HERMAN, a few other people in our family had already shoe stores in Brussels and were making a nice living. So when we got married, Betty's parents paid the rent for a few months for a small store and apartment for us on the rue Haute and they lent us money to buy some ladies' shoes. Rue Haute was a very long, narrow street in a neighborhood called *Les Marolles*. Poor working people were living there. It was near a big square called *Le Grand Sablon*. I hear that now this square is a very fancy place with restaurants and cafés and antique stores.

Our dining room and kitchen were behind the store. We didn't have a living room. In those times, this was not unusual. When people came to visit, you sat around the dining room table. Our table took up almost the whole room. The kitchen was right behind — there was no door in between. The dining room didn't have a window; the kitchen did, but it looked out on a wall in a courtyard. Betty cooked on a coal stove that was next to the window. A lot of times we would eat dinner at her parents' house. Betty was too busy with the store to have much time for cooking. Also cooking didn't interest her too much.

Today they sell stoves in antique stores just like the one we had in our kitchen. They get hundreds of dollars for them. I like nice modern furniture. Maybe I lived too long with old stuff. Our two small bedrooms upstairs also had old furniture.

We had a toilet between the floors off a narrow circular staircase. Once a week we went to the public bathhouse that was across the street not very far from us — the same bathhouse where Emma found out the truth about the letter. The rest of the time we washed with wash cloths in the kitchen or we used pitchers filled with water and the big wide bowls that we kept upstairs in our bedroom, on top of our chest of drawers.

Most of the time we were sitting around the dining-room table waiting for customers. We had a few cousins who had moved to Brussels from Przedborz, and they were living in the same neighborhood. Mostly they were selling things in the *Marché aux Puces* [flea market] which was not far from us. Sometimes they would drop in. I enjoyed having a cup of tea and sitting and talking with them. Betty thought it was a lot of gossip and silly talk. She preferred to read a book or to knit and sometimes she was doing both. When someone came into the store a bell rang and one of us would run out.

In 1932, a few months after our son Joe was born — in those days before we came to America we called him Jojo or Yossele — I got a letter from my mother. "Fella is lying in bed too much; there is nothing for her to do here in Klucze. She is very unhappy. She loves little children. If you sent for her, she could help you and Betty take care of Yossele. Maybe you could even find a match for her in Belgium." I talked it over with Betty and we sent papers for Fella to come to Belgium.

A few months later, Betty and I were upstairs already in bed, when we heard a woman yelling on the street. First we didn't pay attention, but the yelling continued, so I started to listen. I realized she was yelling, "Henyek, your sister is here!" We ran downstairs and opened the door and there was Fella standing with a suitcase. We didn't have a telephone at this time, so she couldn't tell us that she was coming a day early. We gave her something to eat. I asked her about everyone in Poland, and then we took her upstairs. We had already put a bed for her in the room with the baby. She looked at Joe,

"Such a beautiful child!" she was saying over and over. She was very tired and she went to sleep. Like my mother said, Fella enjoyed very much taking care of Joe. When the weather was good she took him to a little park, *Le Petit Sablon,* not too far away. Sometimes she took him to visit family. Now if a few customers came into the store at the same time, Betty and I could both go out and take care of them.

◆ ◆ ◆

In the summer of 1933, Betty and Fella took Joe to Klucze for a month to visit. I wanted my family to meet Betty and Joe, and Betty was curious to see Klucze and meet everybody. Even before she met me, she always heard from her father stories about Klucze and my family.

The first morning she was there Betty got up, put on her bathing suit, and jumped into the river. Our house was surrounded by the river, but we never went into the water to swim. Sometimes in the summer we would sit on the bank and get our feet wet, or splash a little water around, but that was all. People didn't go swimming so much in those days. My mother, my sisters, my brother all ran out screaming — "Betty, what are you doing? You could get sick, you could catch pneumonia from such cold water; please get out." She told them not to worry and kept swimming. Betty loved to tell about this; she thought it was very funny.

She also loved to tell how when she was growing up in Fulda, which was on a river, a lot of times she would write notes to her Hebrew School teacher to explain why she would not be able to come to class — she was very good at forging her mother's handwriting and signature — and then she would go swimming in the river. "And that is why I am such a good swimmer, but I don't know any Hebrew," she would always say at the end of the story. She still swims, but now she goes in the pool in our building.

When she came back to Brussels, Betty was saying how beautiful Klucze was and how terrific the river was for going swimming every day. She was also telling everybody that there was no electricity in the house — we had naphtha gas lamps — and no indoor toilet. After a while, I got mad at her and told her to stop. This is how it was in the country in Poland in those days. In the winter, we went in chamber pots and the maids took them to the latrine. Growing up in Germany, she had never seen something like this.

Betty liked very much my family. She was telling everybody how nice and smart everyone was. Especially she liked Balche. "It's hard to believe that Balche and Fella are sisters," she was telling people when Fella was not around. "Balche is afraid of nothing; she has so much energy and enthusiasm. She rides around on her horse and oversees the work that the farmers are doing, but there is not enough for her to do in Klucze. I wish *she* was living in Brussels."

A few years after Betty's visit, Balche got married; she was about thirty years old. I never met her husband, but everybody said he was a very nice man. By then things were beginning to become more modern; a dowry was not so important anymore. Her husband was a photographer and they were living in Czestochowa. He had a studio there. They had a beautiful baby girl — she sent me some pictures. She was in her thirties when they murdered her and her family. Did they take them and shoot them and throw them into a mass grave? Did they take them to a camp and gas them? I don't know and I try not to think about such things, but sometimes I can't help it. This is why I cry.

◆ ◆ ◆

Around the same time as Balche, Jakob also got married. He and his wife Jagda lived in Klucze. They brought in electricity and indoor plumbing; they made a lot of other improvements. They had a radio; they had a car. They had a baby; his name was Josef. Jakob was in his forties when they murdered him and his family. The Nazis came to Klucze to take him away, but he wouldn't go, so they shot him in front of the house.

Balche and her husband's wedding portrait, 1936

Myriam in Klucze on the small island
where the family's home stood, 1967

Yamrus, Henyek's childhood friend in Klucze, 1967

Myriam in Poland in 1967, next to the sign
carrying the name of the small town near Klucze

Joe in Poland in the 1990s next to the sign bearing the family name

How do I know this? In 1967, my daughter Myriam went to Poland. In this time, she was married to Stanley. In Warsaw, they found a Jewish taxi driver who spoke Yiddish — he was translating for them — to take them to Przedborz. When they got there, the driver asked people how to get to Klucze where the Miedzianagora family once lived, but nobody could tell him, or maybe they didn't want to tell him. Finally, they found an old man who sent them on a road going south. They were driving down this road looking for a piece of land and a house in the woods and thinking they will never find it. But then they saw a farmer walking down the road. The driver stopped the car and asked him, "Do you know by any chance, where is a place called Klucze...."

As soon as he heard Klucze, the farmer said, "Of course, I know Klucze! Henyek Miedzianagora and I were friends when we were boys; we used to play together." I couldn't believe it when Myriam came back to Los Angeles and showed me pictures — even after almost forty years I recognized my old friend Yamrus! I was very excited and started to remember our times together, running around in the forest hiding from each other, playing ball, going to the mill and sitting on the river watching the wheel turn.

Myriam told me, "When the cab driver pointed to me and said that I was your daughter, Yamrus was at first speechless, and then very excited. 'Is Henyek still alive?' he asked. When I told him you were alive and well and living in California, he repeated 'California' a few times as if I had told him you had moved to Mars."

So Yamrus got in the taxi and took them to Klucze. He told them that when the Nazis came to get Jakob and his family, Jakob refused to go with them, so they shot him. The Nazis took away his wife Jagda and their son Josef and burned down the house. I have heard that as soon as they came to Przedborz, the Nazis murdered about a thousand Jews and put them in a mass grave, but it was mostly older Jews.

Maybe my brother Moshe is lying in this grave. Jagda and Josef they probably sent to Treblinka to die.

◆ ◆ ◆

Fella lived with us until she married Sam. Betty always said that one of the happiest days in her life was when they got married. "The burden was off my shoulders; I felt light like a feather." Fella and Betty were not a good combination. Betty was very hard-working, never tired, always taking control of everything and everybody. She was hardly ever sick and, when she was, she never wanted to stay in bed. Always she had to be doing something. When she got an idea about something, she could make a decision, even a big decision, in two seconds. She could get done in one hour what it would take other people ten hours. Here in Los Angeles when we are eating at home, she can make a whole dinner in twenty minutes. She likes everything quick. She even found a German *coiffeur* on Sunset Boulevard who cuts her hair in three minutes. I don't think this is possible, but this is what she tells me. For Fella it is hard to even get up in the morning, and her whole life she is complaining that she is sick, that she doesn't feel good. Sometimes I get really annoyed at her; I am sick of hearing her complain all the time. Other times it makes me sad to see her this way. She is a very smart and talented woman, but I think she never got over *tatte* dying and she stayed like a child.

Sam, Fella's husband, was a Polish Jew who immigrated to Canada in the 1920s. He was on his way back from visiting his family in Poland when we met him. He was going to take a boat from Antwerp to Montreal, but instead he married Fella and stayed in Brussels. Sam was not so smart, but he took good care of Fella. We gave him a job working as a salesman in our store.

13

I N 1932, WHEN BETTY and I opened our store, working-class
women were so poor they didn't have any money to buy
nice shoes. They wore sabots, or very heavy ugly shoes, so
this is what we sold. Stylish shoes were only for richer ladies
who went to fancy boot-makers to buy — or to have made
to order — elegant shoes made out of the finest leather. One
morning, maybe six months after we had been in business,
Betty and I were sitting at the table waiting for the bell to ring
and a customer to come in. On the table was an open box of
shoes that Betty had bought that morning to wear to a wedding. Betty was never the kind of woman who likes to spend
a lot of money on clothes and shoes, and is always thinking
about something new to buy. Now she was complaining how
expensive these shoes were and they were not even from the
best boot-makers. "They cost about as much as some of our
customers earn in a month," she said. As she was saying this we
both started to get the same idea: Let's buy some more shoes
from the boot-maker, and take them to the manufacturer in
Iseghem from whom we were buying most of the shoes in our
store. We will ask him to make cheap copies for our customers.
This turned out to be a million-dollar idea. The women were
so happy to have these nice-looking shoes, they were waiting
in line to get into our store.

A few years later we saw an ad in the paper for a store
downtown at 4, rue St. Catherine. Right away we went to take

a look. The store was not very big — but much bigger than our store on rue Haute — you could put maybe ten chairs inside. When we saw that right in front of the door was the stop for all the trams coming from working-class neighborhoods in and around Brussels, we got very excited. We wanted to see the owner right away. We found a public telephone and called the number in the ad. The owner was in his office and he made an appointment for us to come later in the afternoon. We walked around the neighborhood; we went to a restaurant to eat lunch; and then it was time to go and meet Monsieur LaVigne.

He was maybe sixty years old. His office was very big. All the walls were paneled in a very fine wood. The suit he was wearing would probably cost a few thousand dollars today. Monsieur LaVigne was very rich and very friendly. We told him all about our store on rue Haute, how we built up the business, and now we had so many customers we needed a bigger store in a better location. Because we were selling shoes for working-class women, the location on rue St. Catherine was perfect for us. "You are the first people to answer my ad," he said. "I could probably get more money for the store, but I like you; I can see that you are very hard-working and smart, and you can have it."

We were so happy we went to a tea salon on the Grande Place to have patisserie and coffee to celebrate. I always ordered apple tart, and Betty's favorite was a little cake with mocha.

In the evening we went for dinner to Betty's parents. We told them the good news. Abraham opened a bottle of brandy that he made himself, and we drank a toast to our new store. After the toast Betty said, "Listen papa, why don't you take over our store on rue Haute? It's a very good business and much less work than what you are doing. I think it's a very good idea. What do you say?"

"Betty, it is an interesting idea, but I need time to think it over," he answered. "It is true I am getting very tired of making frankfurters and salami. If you took all the salamis and frank-furters I have made in the last twenty-five years and you laid them out on the boulevards that go around Brussels starting right here at the *Boulevard du Midi,* you could probably make a circle around the whole city at least once, probably twice."

We were laughing a lot at this idea. When we stopped, Betty continued, "Shoes you don't have to make, papa; you have only to sell them. It will be a very nice change for you."

"Betty, I don't want to talk about this anymore tonight. I promise you, I will think very seriously about your offer."

The next evening Abraham came to see us. Betty didn't have to say another word. As soon as he came in, he told us he made a decision. He wanted to take over the store. He kept it for many years, and I don't think he ever regretted going from salamis to shoes.

Betty and I were working and spending very little money, and for a while we were the only ones selling nice shoes to poor women. So by the time we rented the store on rue St. Catherine, we had enough money to buy a three-story, brown-brick building on Avenue Coghen in Uccle, one of the most beautiful neighborhoods in Brussels. It was hard for people to believe we had made so much money in so little time. One day my sister Fella told me that she heard some cousins say that we must have won the lottery!

◆ ◆ ◆

We moved into a second-floor apartment in our building in June 1935. Now we had a bathroom and nice size rooms with windows looking out on trees and bushes and gardens.

Avenue Coghen is a wide avenue lined with trees that goes from *Chausée* Bruggeman to *Chausée* d'Alsenbergh. This is where we were living when Myriam was born. We were very happy; now we had a boy and a girl. What could be better? But soon two very bad things happened. About a month after Myriam was born, my mother-in-law Bertha had a surgery — it was for a hernia, nothing very serious. But in those times after a surgery like this, the doctors were telling people to stay in bed for ten days. From lying in bed for so long, she got a blood clot and this is what killed her. She was only fifty-four years old.

Then about three months after Bertha died, Myriam almost died. She was a very healthy baby, but one day our maid asked us if she could bring her little nephew over to play at our house while she was working. "My sister has to go to an interview for a job and she has no one else to leave him with," she told us. We said, "Certainly, bring him." What she did not tell us was that her nephew had whooping cough — they didn't have a vaccination in those days.

Myriam was five months old. She was coughing and coughing and couldn't breathe; she was in an oxygen tent. Betty and I were so worried we didn't sleep one night. The doctor told us he was not sure if she would make it. Thank God, she did make it. And she was not so sick again until we were living in Morocco.

14

BETTY AND I WERE working very hard in our store and Fella who took care of Joe was going to get married, so I brought over from Przedborz a distant cousin of mine, Golda Cliska, to take care of Myriam and Joe. Golda's family was very poor and she was happy to come and live with us. Golda was not very tall, a little bit overweight, not so good-looking, but a nice face with dark curly hair. A person as sweet and kind as her you rarely see. She was so good to the children, always singing to them — in Yiddish, in Polish, in French — and hugging and kissing them, and they were crazy about her. When Myriam was two-and-a-half years old, Golda got married to Henri Cohen, a Moroccan Jew.

One day Henri had come into our store and asked to speak to the owners. He told me and Betty that he was a very good salesman with a lot of experience in Morocco. He had just immigrated to Belgium and needed a job. We both liked him right away, and we could see that he had the right personality for sales. We needed more help, so we hired him. Through us, he met Golda and a year later they got married and Golda stopped working for us. We needed someone to live with us; a lot of times we didn't get back from the store until close to eight at night. But we always saw the children for a few hours in the daytime. In Europe, everybody used to go home from work for lunch. This is when we had our big meal.

Henyek with Joe and Myriam at the beach

Fella and Golda on an outing with Joe

Portrait of Golda

The last day Golda was taking care of them, the children already knew she was not coming back. Betty and I came home from the store earlier than usual. Golda kissed the children and hugged and hugged them so many times, and then she opened the door to leave. But they — especially Myriam — were screaming and crying and holding onto her skirt so she couldn't get out. We knew that Myriam would be very upset — Joe was already going to school, so it was not as bad for him — but we did not think it would be this terrible. I can still see the whole scene like it happened yesterday.

Betty told Golda not to come to visit the children for three months. This way Myriam would forget her and would quickly get used to Gertrude, the German woman that Betty hired. This is what Betty thought and she always made the decisions about the children. Gertrude was a nice lady, but not the same like Golda.

In July 1943, the Nazis sent Golda and her husband to Auschwitz and gassed them. After the war someone who was in the same convoy and came back, told us that when the Nazis came to pick up Golda, they did not have papers to take Henri — he was a French citizen and they were not yet deporting French Jews. But he didn't want Golda to go alone. He thought they would be working together in Germany, so he went with her!

Not too long after Golda came to live with us and take care of the children, we moved again. We bought a nice big piece of land also on Avenue Coghen, but closer to Avenue Bruggeman, and we put up a five-story apartment building with an elevator that looked very much like the one I was so excited about in my sister Yochitl's apartment house in Warsaw. There were two apartments on each floor, but for our apartment we took the whole second floor, so we had twelve rooms — double the size of the other apartments. Instead of having a dining room and a living room separated by one big arch, we had four rooms separated by arches, with two sets of bay windows overlooking the street. It was such a big space, you could invite fifty people and it wasn't crowded. I have always liked big living rooms. In Los Angeles, our dining room and living room together are twenty-six feet long by eighteen wide. During the war, it was a different story. In Morocco, all four of us slept and lived in one room for six months. In New York, for five years, Betty and I slept on the convertible couch in a living room that was maybe twelve by twelve feet. We were lucky just to be alive.

For our new apartment, we bought beautiful Persian carpets for the front rooms, and the best new furniture you could find. Now they call this furniture art deco style and they write books about it. One of the rooms was my office and I had a big, shiny, cherrywood desk in the corner facing out. I needed the desk because I took care of all the finances for our business. I enjoyed this. Betty didn't like anything that had to do with accounting. She was very happy that we were making such a good living and she was very proud of our beautiful new apartment, but she had no interest in knowing any details about our finances. Most of the time, she didn't even know how much we had in the bank, or how much we were making every month. When the war started, she didn't know I had so much money hidden in the apartment — just in case we needed to get out of Europe. Betty was very good in making decisions about the business. She always figured out the right shoes to buy and how many to order, and she used to make a very nice window display. Together we had everything you need for success in business.

Our three bedrooms had big doors that opened up on a terrace that was the width of the building, with stairs going down to a very long rectangular garden with apple and pear trees, and bushes with red currants and gooseberries. I have never seen these fruit in the U.S. I have never seen apples and pears as big as the ones in our garden. Each one was two or three times the normal size. One time after the war when we were living in Brussels — it was maybe 1947 — Joe and I took a few apples and pears with us when we went to New York. We wanted to show them to our friends. But when the customs inspectors saw them they told us it was against the law to bring foreign fruit into the United States. We were very upset and very quick we took a few bites before they took the fruit from us.

Soon after we moved into 242 Avenue Coghen, I said to Betty that I would like to bring my mother and Rifke over from Poland to live with us. My mother had problems with her heart and I thought that in Brussels we could get better doctors to take care of her than in the country in Poland. Betty liked my mother very much and she said "yes." Rifke was a poor Jewish girl from Przedborz and she was living in Klucze with my mother, helping to take care of her.

The doctors in Brussels helped my mother a lot and she was happy living with us. Sometimes she would go with Golda and take the children to *Parc* Wolvendael to play. The park was less than ten minutes from our house, but sometimes even this was too much for her, so they would take a little walk on Avenue Coghen. Across the street from us was the entrance to the College St. Pierre, a fancy Catholic high school for boys. On one side of our building was a big empty lot where the children were playing, and on the other side a one-family house where the Schoerman family lived. They were very nice people — he was a baron — and they had three children, Yves, Roger, and Ginette. Joe and Myriam used to play with them.

After the war, Madame Schoerman came to see us and she gave us an envelope. Inside were some of our family pictures. She told us that in 1940, a few months after we ran away, she was hiding behind the drapes in her living room watching the German soldiers carry our personal things out of our apartment to make room for a general. "I was so upset when I saw them carrying boxes with your photo albums," she said, "and I could see some of the pictures falling down, I wanted to run out and pick them up, but I knew they could put me in prison or even kill me if I did. After they left, I waited a little bit and then I went outside to see if there were any pictures lying in the gutter; there were only a few. They are in this envelope."

Part III

WORLD WAR II

How My Family and I Escaped from Europe
and Came to America

15

FOR US, THE WAR started on May 10, 1940, around five o'clock in the morning. We were sound asleep, when all of a sudden we heard noises so loud we both jumped out of bed.

"Maybe it's thunder?" Betty said. She was sitting up on the bed. I was already walking to the balcony door.

"Believe me, it's not thunder," I told her.

When you grow up on a farm, you know exactly the sound of thunder. I pulled on the drawstrings to open the heavy drapes that kept out the light. I opened the door and walked out on the terrace. Betty was already next to me. The sky was covered with planes dropping bombs. Betty said only one German word "*krieg*" and she started to shiver. I understood why she said this word. She had told me once that in 1914 when she was five years old she was playing in front of her house in Offenbach with some other children when they heard people talking very loud and excited and they were saying, "*Krieg! Krieg! Es ist krieg!*" [War! War! The war has started!]. She had no idea what this word meant, but she thought that it must be something very important and wonderful, so she ran into her house very happy to tell this news. She was running around looking for her mother yelling "*Muttee! Muttee! Krieg! Krieg!*" Now she knew exactly what "*krieg*" meant.

We went quickly to the living room and turned on the radio. We heard "*pour la deuxième fois en trente ans, les boches ont attaqué La Belgique*" [For the second time in thirty years, the Huns have attacked Belgium"]. We were concentrating so hard on what they were saying about the attack, we didn't even notice when my mother walked in a few minutes later. "What is it?" she asked. "The terrible noise woke me up."

We turned around and saw her in her robe, leaning on her cane, and looking very scared. Next to her was standing Rifke. When we told them what was happening, my mother sat down and she was burying her head in her hands. "*Oy vey is mir! Noch a mool krieg*" [Woe is me! Again a war]. She kept repeating "*Noch a mool krieg! Noch a mool krieg!*" (When Betty said "*krieg*" she was speaking German; when my mother said "*krieg,*" she was speaking Yiddish.) While my mother was sitting moaning and crying, we heard the children walking down the hallway to the living room. We were thinking maybe they would sleep through the bombing — with little children, you can be banging on the wall with a hammer next to their bed and it won't wake them up — but after a while even they heard the bombs.

"I looked out the door to the terrace and the sky is filled with planes and bombs falling," Joe said.

He was sounding more excited than scared — he was only eight years old, too young to understand how dangerous it was. Myriam was three years old and she didn't understand what was happening, only that it was something bad. I could see that she was going to start crying, so I took her on my lap and we continued to listen to the radio. After a few minutes, the announcer said that the government wants everybody who owns a car to bring it to the caserne for the army. It wasn't even a year since we had bought a beautiful new 1939 Ford. Betty and I looked at each other.

"How will we get to La Panne if we give the car to the army?" she asked.

We were already talking about going to the seashore to get away from the bombing. La Panne was the closest town to the French border.

"I think we have to do what the government asks," I said.

"You are not answering my question. How will we get to La Panne without a car?"

"We will get a taxi," I said. "We have phone numbers of a few good companies — the ones that pick up Fella or your father when they are visiting and have to go home late at night."

"We will probably never see the car again if we give it to the army." She was shaking her head and letting out a loud breath, as if it was a very stupid idea to give them the car.

This argument was the opposite of how it was usually. Betty grew up in Germany, so most of the time she wanted to follow the rules, and I was more ready to go around the rules.

But now it was wartime and she didn't care.

"If the army needs cars to help fight the Germans, then we have to give them the car," I said. "And how will it look for our Belgian citizenship, if they find out that we didn't follow a government order?"

"You really think the Belgian army will stop Hitler!" This idea made her laugh. "You are dreaming. Only the French army and the Maginot Line can stop the Germans; and if they can't stop them, then we will really need the car."

In the end, I won the argument, and later on I regretted it very much.

Betty got dressed and took the car to the caserne. When she came back, she said that the line to get a receipt was so long that she just left the car there with the key in the ignition and walked away. She was very angry. "Are you happy now?" she asked me.

By eight o'clock I was at the *Banque Nationale de Belgique* to take out some money. There were already hundreds of people waiting in line; in the meantime, the Germans are dropping bombs. Everybody is looking up at the sky; I hear women in the line praying "*Jésus, Marie, aidez nous,*" and

"*Notre père qui êtes aux cieux....*" After about twenty minutes, I am thinking, "To hell with the money, we've got to get
away from here right away." I had a few thousand dollars,
some Belgian francs, and a few pieces of jewelry hidden at
home for an emergency.

Besides this, in 1936, I sent $10,000 to First National City
Bank in New York. Sure, like most people I thought Hitler was
a *michugana,* but I was not so sure the German people would
get rid of him. I read the newspapers, I listened to the radio, I
heard his speeches, and I was scared. I knew how stupid people
can be especially when they are poor and suffering, how they
believe anything their leaders tell them, even when the leaders
are crazy or make up crazy stories. In Poland, the Catholic
priests were telling the people that at Passover we Jews kill
Christian babies and use their blood to make *matzohs* and the
people believed them, so why wouldn't the Germans believe
Hitler, and continue to support him?

Betty didn't think that such an educated, cultured people
would stick with Hitler. The German Jews were such patriots.
Her brother's middle name was Wilhelm, after the Kaiser (it
didn't help him in Auschwitz), and all the men on her mother's
side were in the army in World War I. We still have pictures
they sent to her parents. They are standing in their uniforms,
so proud to be fighting for the *Vaterland.* It didn't help them
either. We Polish Jews knew better; we knew that most of the
Polish people hated us and we could not trust them.

◆ ◆ ◆

Betty had telephoned her father and my sister Fella to come
over and come to the seashore with us, so by the time I came
home, everybody was sitting around the dining room table
eating rolls with butter, drinking coffee, and looking worried.
I sat down and took a cup of coffee and a roll. I had been
up for close to four hours and I had smoked maybe a dozen
cigarettes, but this was the first food I put in my mouth. I told
them what happened at the bank.

"How will we have enough money then? Especially if the situation gets worse?" Betty asked me.

"Don't worry, we'll have enough. I will explain it to you later," I answered her. I didn't want to tell her in front of everyone exactly how much money — and diamonds — I had hidden in the apartment. I was shaking my head just a little bit from side to side, so that she would understand not to ask me again in front of everybody.

"You are the finance minister," she said. "If you are not worried, then I am not worried. While you were gone, I called a taxi company and ordered the biggest car they have for ten o'clock to take all of us to La Panne."

"Why do we have to go to La Panne, why can't we go to Coq Sur Mer like we always do in the summer?" Joe asked.

I didn't want to tell him that just in case things got very bad, it was better to be next to the French frontier, so I told him, "I heard that La Panne is even nicer than Coq Sur Mer."

"I want to go to Coq Sur Mer," Myriam said. "I want to go to the beach and get wet in the water."

"La Panne has a nice beach, too, and you can go in the water there if it's warm enough," Betty told her.

"No, I want to go to Coq Sur Mer, like we always do," Myriam repeated again.

"Listen, we are not going to Coq Sur Mer, so be quiet! I don't want to hear about Coq Sur Mer anymore," Betty told her.

"Myriam, come with me," Fella said. "I will help you to get dressed to go to the seashore," and she took her to the bedroom and we had a few minutes of quiet.

We were still hoping that the Maginot Line and the Albert canal would keep the Germans out and that we would be back in a few days, so we just threw a few things into overnight bags, and by ten o'clock we were in the taxi going north to La Panne.

It was a big car with the extra little seats that you pull down in the back. Still it was very crowded — me, Betty, my mother, Rifke, my sister Fella, and Abraham, Betty's father. The children sat on our laps.

We were driving for a while when all of a sudden we heard planes. We got out of Brussels to get away from the bombing, but now we looked up and saw German planes flying low in our direction. There were very few cars on the road and it would have been very easy for them to pick us out. Before we even had a chance to say a word, the taxi driver stopped the car.

"We better run and hide in those wheat fields," he said, and right away he opened his door and got out. And this is what we did. Betty grabbed Joe; I was carrying Myriam. Abraham and Rifke helped my mother get out, and even Fella ran fast to hide in the field. The planes went right over us. We could hear bombs exploding and we saw fires not so far away. After about twenty minutes it was quiet. We got back into the taxi and started to drive again toward a little town called Waregem. Close by was an airport and the Germans tried to bomb it, but they missed and most of the damage was to the town. We drove into Waregem and saw houses burning and dead horses lying on the road. We saw wounded people with blood all over their clothes. An old lady was screaming. Her hair was burnt off. The bombs made a very big hole — I think you call this a crater — in the road, so it was very hard to get through.

Myriam started to cry. "I want to go home," she said. All through France and Spain, she was saying all the time, "I want to go home" and "I want my bed." At this time she still believed us when we said, "We will go home in a few days." Later on, she knew it wasn't true and after a while we stopped saying it. We were going further and further away from her bed and from home.

We made it through Waregem and got to La Panne. It was before the summer, so it was easy to find a villa to rent. We carried in our few bags, and then we went to a small restaurant very close to get some lunch. The minute we walked in, Myriam yelled out, "Look! Look! Mireille." Sitting at a table in the corner was Betty's first cousin Golda — this was a different Golda from the one who took care of Myriam and Joe — her husband Henrico and their little girl. Mireille was just a little younger than Myriam and they used to play together.

We were very happy to see each other. The waiter put a few tables together — we were eight adults and three children — and we all sat down. Golda and Henrico had the same idea like us. "We came to La Panne to get away from the bombing and get close to France just in case...," they told us. But they were smarter than us; they didn't give away their car to the Belgian army. After this, we were spending a lot of time together. We were sitting all day in the living room of our villa, listening to the radio.

After a few days, Henrico told us, "Tomorrow morning I am going back to Brussels. I have to take money out of the bank. We only have enough for a few weeks."

When Betty's father heard this, right away he said, "I am going back with you. I have nothing here, not even a pajama."

Abraham had come with us only because Betty had insisted so much. Now she was begging him, "Listen papa, don't go, stay with us. We have plenty of money; we will buy you a pajama. We will buy you whatever you need." He didn't say anything; this was in the evening.

Early the next morning, we heard a noise. Betty got out of bed and opened the door and she saw her father — with his shoes in his hands — walking down the stairs. She ran after him.

"Papa, why are you going? Please, please don't go." She was speaking to him in German.

"Betty, I have to go; I must make my own decision."

Even Betty could not get him to change his mind. He gave her a big hug and got in the car and Henrico took him back to Brussels. A few days later, Henrico came back, but not Abraham.

The next time Betty saw her father was in 1946. He was lucky — he had blue eyes and light color hair so the Germans did not think he was Jewish. He got a false *carte d'identité* and he made it through the war. His son Julius was not so lucky.

Julius got married the day before the war began — on May 9th. Later on, Betty always said, "If only he had not gotten married, he would still be alive; he was like my child. I would have made sure he came with us."

He would also have been alive if he had jumped off the truck that was taking him to Auschwitz. After the war, two of his friends came and told us that they were in the same convoy. Before they got into Germany, when the truck slowed down a little, they jumped off. The whole war they were hiding and they made it. They were begging Julius to jump with them, but he told them: "I don't want to take a chance, I could break a leg or an arm. I prefer to go and work in Germany for a few years." Who could imagine Auschwitz?

The bombing started on a Friday. It was a holiday weekend and we were hoping that by Tuesday we will be back in Brussels. We heard Paul Reynaud, the French prime minister, on the radio. He was saying all the time, *"Nous sommes forts et nous vaincrons"* [We are strong and we shall win]. The French had the Maginot Line and an army of 800,000 men. The Belgian prime minister said, *"Nous avons le canal Albert; ils ne passeront pas"* [We have the Albert canal, and they will not pass]. But by Sunday, the German army was already around Namur overlooking the Meuse river. By Tuesday, they were in Brussels, and we decided to go to France. But how could we leave? We had given our car to the Belgian army.

"A Nazi is probably driving our car by now," Betty told me. "Why did I listen to you? I was so stupid. I should have kept the car." She was right. It was a terrible mistake to give it away, but I didn't enjoy hearing this over and over, or looking at her angry face.

We started going to garages and asking if they had a car for sale. The answer was always "no," but finally we got lucky. One man told me, "I don't have anything for you, but my brother-in-law, Roger, has a garage a little bit out of town in

Leaving the Brussels Town Hall after Julius's marriage ceremony;
next to him is Joe. Myriam is holding the bride Mari's hand.
Behind Julius is his father Abraham. Henyek is behind the bride;
behind him is Henrico, and behind Henrico is his wife, Golda.
Betty is in the center back wearing a large hat.

the direction of Furnes. Yesterday, one of his clients bought a new car and Roger bought his old Ford from him."

Right away, I took a taxi to this garage. (Betty and Golda were in the park with the children.) When I got there, I found only a very young boy working on a car.

"Oh *Meneer* Vandervelde won't be back for at least another hour; he is home having lunch," he told me.

"His brother-in-law told me that he has a Model T Ford for sale. Can I take a look at it?"

"It's in the back, I'll show you, but I think he might already have sold it. Someone came in early this morning."

When he saw the look on my face, he said, "I'm not sure about this. I am just an apprentice learning to be a car mechanic; it's possible the man didn't offer him the right price."

It was a good thing I only had two cigarettes left on me. I could have smoked a whole pack until Roger came back. Finally, he arrived. Right away I saw that he was driving the exact same 1939 Ford we gave to the army; this made me feel sick. But then I got some good news.

"The fellow who came this morning couldn't afford the car," he told me. "I don't know why he even came to look at it. Just dreaming, I guess. So many people dream of owning their own car." He shrugged his shoulders. He was a very tall, thin man maybe in his fifties, but he still had a full head of light brown hair combed back very straight and shiny with a lot of pomade. "This 1932 Model T Ford that you are interested in is in very good condition. I can take you for a short ride, if you like."

I was so desperate I would have bought the car as long as the motor started, but I said, "*Dat zou heel goed zyn. Dankuwel* [That would be very good. Thank you], and he drove me around for a few minutes. We were in *Flandres*, so Roger was speaking to me in Flemish and I was trying to answer him back in Flemish. In Belgium, the French and the Flemish people don't like each other so much. When I moved to Brussels, it was easy for me to learn some Flemish because it is like Yiddish — a dialect of German — and so a lot of words are the same.

As soon as we got back to the garage, we agreed on a price. I think it was five thousand francs, and I told him I would come back that evening with the money and my wife — Betty was the driver.

In 1935, when we bought our first car, I had learned how to drive, too, but one time I made a bad mistake and we almost had an accident. "How could you do something so stupid?" Betty was yelling. "You almost killed us." After that, she was always very nervous and criticizing me when I was driving and this made me very nervous. So finally I told her, "I would be very happy for you to be my chauffeur." And from that day on, for about thirty-five years, I never drove a car.

When we came back, Roger told us, "You are very lucky. Just a few hours after you were here, some other people also from Brussels and also running from the *boches* came and offered me much more money for the car, but I told them that I had promised it to you, and I could not go back on my word." He gave us the car for the price we agreed on. He was a very decent man.

The next problem was — no gasoline. Roger said, "Maybe there is a tiny bit in the bottom of the gas-station pump." So we squeezed out a few liters. Enough to get started. We drove back to the villa and the next morning we crossed over into France. It was maybe seven days after we left Brussels. (On May 27 — only seventeen days after we left Brussels — Belgium asked for an armistice and the German occupation started.) There was no problem crossing the border; the French *gendarme* waved to us to go. We were traveling together with Golda, Henrico, and Mireille. Either we followed them or they followed us.

16

SOMETIMES WHEN I TELL this story, people say, "How could you drive for weeks and weeks in hot weather with five adults and two children in a Model T Ford?" When you have no choice, you manage. Fella, my mother, and Rifke sat in the back and they were taking turns holding Myriam on their laps. They had a hard job to keep her from complaining and crying. They were telling stories, singing songs, letting her comb their hair. Joe was mostly sitting on my lap in the front, but sometimes we switched around. He was eight years old and so happy that he didn't have to go to school. His school in Uccle was very strict and he did not like it. So, for him, running from Hitler was exciting, an adventure. He says he was not scared. (His wife and his daughter say that he repressed his fear and this is why he is so nervous about a lot of things. I don't know. I don't understand psychology.)

Joe was looking out the window all the time, and even an eight-year-old child could see that we were the lucky ones. On the roads were thousands and thousands of refugees going south. Some were in cars like us — a lot of them had mattresses, blankets, furniture, baby carriages, and other stuff tied around the roof — some were in carts pulled by horses, some were on bicycles, but many more were walking and carrying knapsacks, suitcases, babies.

In the other direction were tanks and armored trucks of the French and English army going toward Dunkirk on the border of Belgium. The English troops were holding their thumbs up — saying "We will get them." Everybody was still thinking that in a short time the English and French would push the Germans back and we could go back home. But just in case everybody was wrong, I had ten thousand dollars (plus some interest; it was more than three years already since I sent the money) sitting at the First National City Bank in New York City.

One of our first stops in France was in Amiens. We went to a nice restaurant — a few days ago, more than forty years later, Joe told me what he ate there. "It was some kind of veal with a delicious French mustard sauce; I still remember the taste." Probably he remembers it because we did not have too many wonderful meals after that.

◆ ◆ ◆

That same night we drove to a small town called Peronne and got rooms in a hotel. The children slept with us. My mother, Fella, and Rifke were together in another room. I brought in what little luggage we had, and then we took turns washing up. In those days you were lucky if a hotel in a small town had even one bathroom for the whole place. The toilet was always out in the hallway. Betty washed out some clothes and put them to dry in our room, and then we went down to the restaurant for dinner. When we walked in, we saw that they were cooking in wrought-iron pots hanging over a fireplace that took up almost a whole wall. Each log of wood was maybe six feet long. The pots were as big as the ones we used in the Polish army to cook for the men in our barracks. The children never saw anything like this before and they were very excited about it. "It looks just like the Middle Ages," Joe said. He was already learning some history in school. I had to run after Myriam all the time because she was running over to the fireplace and we were afraid she would get burned. We were happy when they finally brought us our food. We ate our dinner and then we got out of there and went to sleep.

Betty and I were waking up a lot during the night — we were rolling all the time into the center of our bed. We were very lucky that we had such a terrible bed; because of it we woke up very early the next morning. We had brought a little radio with us and we turned it on. We heard that the Germans were only about twenty kilometers away. Their panzers broke through the French lines and were going toward Dunkirk. We jumped out of bed and woke everybody up and told them we had to leave right away. We tried not to show the children how scared we were. It took maybe twenty minutes and we were all in the car. But we had a problem. Golda and Henrico were staying at another hotel and we didn't know where. They were supposed to come to our hotel much later, but we couldn't wait. We had to find them very fast. It was so early in the morning, there was no one at the reception desks.

So we started to drive up and down the streets sticking our heads out of the car windows yelling "Golda, Henrico." It was a small town and, after we drove down the main streets, we got worried. Probably they were still asleep and they wouldn't hear us; maybe their room was in the back of the hotel. Or maybe they rented a room in somebody's house? We didn't see their car anywhere.

Next to the last hotel we drove by, there was a café that was already open, so I said to Betty, "Make a u-turn. I'll go into that café and ask if there are any more hotels on the side streets, or if any people rent out rooms." We made the u-turn and, just as we got to the hotel, we heard Golda yelling, "Betty! Henyek! What is going on?" We looked up and saw Golda in her nightgown at the window on the second floor. "I was asleep," she said. "I thought I must be dreaming that someone is yelling for me and Henrico."

"You were not dreaming," I told her. "The Germans are only about twenty kilometers away. We have to get out very fast."

"Henrico and Mireille are still asleep," she said. "But don't worry, we will be downstairs in ten minutes." And they were.

Their car was parked on a side street. They got in and we all went south. Now there were even more people on the roads. The Germans had figured out how to get around the Maginot Line and everybody was trying to get away from them.

The Maginot Line went from around Basel in Switzerland to Montmédy near the Belgian border, but it stopped south of the Ardennes mountains. The French didn't think the Germans could go through the mountains. The Ardennes are not very high, maybe like the Catskills, but usually an army does not try to advance through mountains and forests. But this is exactly what the Germans did — they went through the Ardennes — and they made it. They got into France and now they were a few kilometers from us. After a while they cut off Dunkirk and trapped 250,000 British troops. If we had not left Peronne when we did, we could have been trapped, too.

Gasoline was now rationed in France, and we had to use tricks. When we got to a gas station, the man would ask, "Do you have your rationing stamps?" We would say, "Yes, of course we do." So he would fill up the gas tank. When it came time to pay we had the money ready and then the guy would say, "Where are your stamps?" Betty would answer, "Oh, let me get them," and she would look through her bag — it was a big, beige leather bag with many pockets, compartments, zippers — and make a big fuss. "Oh my God, where are the stamps? Where are the rationing stamps?" She would take everything out and then she would say, "I just can't find them. Somebody must have stolen them." She did this so good I was thinking she could have been an actress. The gas station guys got very upset, but what could they do? Take the gas out of the car? We gave them a nice tip and we left. For a while, I was calling Betty "Sarah Bernhardt" — this was a very famous French actress of the nineteenth century. Everything was so bad, it was good to laugh a little.

We kept going very slowly in the direction of Toulouse. Most of the time the Germans were just fifty or a hundred kilometers behind us. They were advancing very fast and the traffic

was getting slower and slower. The roads were two lanes —
they didn't have highways in those days — and the French kept
the other side for the troops going north. Sometimes we could
only drive a few kilometers in a day.

The further south we went, the hotter it got. By the time
we got to Central France, it was already June. Myriam kept
saying "It's too hot here," and still repeating over and over,
"I want my bed; I want to go home." My mother was trying
not to make trouble, but I could hear from the way she was
breathing and sighing that she was not feeling good. Rifke
was trying to help her; she had a wet washcloth to wipe her
forehead, but after a while the cloth got warm and filled with
sweat. Fella was complaining all the time, "*Oy vey is mir*; it's
so hot I feel like I am going to faint." When I looked over at
Betty, I could see that Fella was getting her very angry. After a
few days of listening to her complain, she said, "What do you
think, Fella, that you are the only one in this car who is hot?
We are all hot — my dress is soaked with sweat — but we are
not complaining all the time like you. Stop it already. I can't
stand it anymore." Fella got very offended and they didn't talk
to each other.

I was soaking wet, too, and nervous and tired of hearing
Fella complain. It was a good thing that cigarettes were so
hard to get, or I would have smoked a few packs a day. Also,
after weeks and weeks in the car, I was bored — there were
no car radios and tapes like you have now — but I was trying
to stay calm, not to complain too much. I didn't need that my
wife and my sister should not be talking to each other. In the
evening, I told Betty, "You are right about Fella, but you know
she is like a child. I want you to make up with her."

"I will make up with her, if you promise me that you —
all of you — are not going to speak Polish anymore." Betty
didn't like it that sometimes when we didn't want the children
to understand, my mother, Fella, Rifke, and I were talking in
Polish. The children didn't understand, but she didn't either.

I promised her and after that we were speaking much less Polish. Every time someone in the back of the car started to speak in Polish, I said, "*Yiddish ou Français, s'il vous plait.*" After a few days, Betty said something nice to Fella and they started talking again.

At night the problem was to find a place to sleep. It was so crowded, some people were sleeping in parks, or on the grass along some of the roads; some were even sleeping on the sidewalks — they put down their heads on their suitcases — and some were sleeping in their cars. We never had to sleep in the car, but sometimes when the restaurants and cafés were full we bought some bread and cheese, or whatever food we could get, and we were sitting in the car and eating, or if we were near a park that was not too crowded we would sit on the grass or a bench and eat.

Sometimes we got lucky at night and found hotel rooms. Sometimes we went to the Red Cross and they would try to find us a private home. Because my mother was old and in bad health, I think they tried harder to help us. Sometimes we slept in schoolyards or in a school gymnasium with hundreds of other refugees. Sometimes farmers let us sleep in their barns. We paid them something.

One night we were sleeping on the hay with the chickens and the other animals. I was up the whole night chasing mice and rats. Around four in the morning, I see the farmer coming towards the barn.

"I was drinking my coffee and listening to the radio, and I have come to tell you that you should leave right away." He was talking like someone who has laryngitis — he already had a cigarette in his hand — but I figured out what he was saying.

"Why? What did you hear?"

"*Les boches*; they are about twenty-five kilometers from here."

I thanked him for telling me and then I woke up Betty. She was sound asleep and I had to shake her a lot before she opened her eyes.

"What's the matter? What's the matter?" she asked. She could see I looked very scared.

"The farmer just came to warn us that the German army is about twenty-five kilometers from here. He heard it on the radio."

Right away Betty started to yell, "Listen everybody, we have to get up and leave very fast."

"I don't want to get the children scared," I whispered to her. "We'll tell them that the farmer came and told us that it is going to be very, very hot today, so we better leave right away." To my mother, Fella, and Rifke I told the truth — in Polish. We were all sleeping in our clothes, so it just took us a few minutes to get out. When we got in the car, we were picking the hay off our hair and our clothes.

This time it was easy to find Golda and her family; they were staying in the next barn on the same road as us.

◆ ◆ ◆

A few days later, we were on the road behind Henrico. The French tanks and trucks had just passed, so the other side of the road was open, but everybody was in the right lane going slowly. Suddenly Henrico gets out of the lane and starts to drive on the opposite side of the road.

"What is he doing? What is he doing?" Betty yelled out, but then she pulled out and followed him.

"Betty, are you crazy?" I was screaming. "The people are going to kill us."

"I just did it," she said. "I didn't have time to think."

The people didn't kill us, but they were honking and screaming at us when we passed them. We were all very scared. In the back of the car everyone was yelling, "What is he doing? Why are you following him?" Myriam started crying. Only Joe was quiet. Later he told us he thought it was exciting! Henrico kept going and Betty kept following. It was maybe four or five kilometers before another military convoy started approaching, and we squeezed back in the right lane. The people had no choice; they had to let us in to make room for the convoy. It saved probably a few hours of driving — we passed hundreds, maybe a thousand cars. But I was very happy when we got back in the right lane.

"I don't care what Henrico does, I don't want you to ever do this again," I told Betty. "I am worried and nervous enough; I don't need more trouble."

Later on when we stopped and got out of our cars, I was yelling at Henrico, "Why did you do such a crazy dangerous thing? What is wrong with you?"

"I just couldn't stand it anymore, going two kilometers an hour."

"The next time you do something like that, I guarantee you we are not going to follow you."

"I won't do it again. Don't worry." And he didn't do it again, at least not while we were together.

We were traveling together for a long time with Henrico and Golda, then when we got close to Gaillac, a small town in Southern France, another strange thing happened. This time Betty was going first and all of a sudden she says, "Where are Golda and Henrico? I don't see their car. They were right behind us a few minutes ago and now I can't see them." She kept looking in the rearview mirror, but they had disappeared.

The next time we saw them was more than a year later in New York! "I made a mistake," Henrico told us. "I don't remember how it happened, but I made a left turn and we went to a town called Albi and then we could not find you again." We were never sure if it was really a mistake. Maybe he thought we were slowing him down because we had so many people with us? We were five adults and two children. They were two adults and one child. It was harder for us to find a place to sleep every night. We will never know.

17

IT WAS LATE IN June when we came to Gaillac, a town about fifty kilometers from Toulouse. We rented a furnished apartment with three small bedrooms in an old white-washed building. For the first time since we left Belgium, we had a kitchen; we could make something to eat. There was not too much further to go in France — the Spanish border was only about one hundred kilometers away. My mother wasn't feeling good; she needed a rest. We all needed a rest from being in the car together from morning to night. Betty and I had to figure out what to do next. We stayed in Gaillac maybe a month or six weeks — we even signed Joe up in school, but he only went for a few days.

Everything was happening so fast. We could see that the French didn't have anymore a strong will to fight. In World War I close to one and a half million French soldiers were killed and many millions were wounded. It was only twenty-two years since that war was over, and almost a million French women were war widows. Probably they didn't want to lose their sons the same way they lost their husbands. By June 14, Paris fell. By June 22, the French and Germans signed an armistice, and some of the French government ran away to North Africa. France got divided into two parts. The Northern part was occupied by the Germans, and the Southern part was run by the French Vichy government. *Maréchal* Petain — a big hero from World War I — was the head. So the war between

France and Germany was over and France lost. How could
we be sure that after a while the Germans wouldn't come into
Southern France, too? Vichy was a puppet government and
Germany was the boss. People were starting to think that the
Germans could win the war.

One evening — it was just around the time when the French
surrendered — Betty and I were walking in the street in Gaillac
with another refugee couple. We left the children at home with
Fella, Rifke, and my mother. After a while we wanted to sit
down in a café and get something to drink. The weather was
very hot and we were looking for a table to sit outside, but
the cafés were very crowded. We kept walking and looking for
one with an empty table. All of a sudden, I see some people
are waving to us. Our friends were busy talking with Betty and
they didn't notice. I interrupted them: "There are some people
in this café waving at us. I don't know them; they must be your
friends." They took a look and right away they were smiling
and waving back. "They are friends of ours from Antwerp,
Monsieur et Madame Faszczak. Let's go sit down with them."
(In Europe, unless you know a person for a long time and you
are very good friends, you always call them by their last name.
It is hard for me, in America, even after so many years to get
used to everybody, even strangers, calling me "Henry" — this
is my American name. Betty and I have dinner maybe three
times a week at Norm's restaurant, and we always have the
same nice waitress who is maybe twenty years old. Always she
asks me, "So what will it be for you today, Henry?")

When they said that name "Faszczak," Betty and I both
remembered that maybe a year before, we got a letter from
my brother Jakob in Poland. He was writing, "My wife Jagda
has an uncle in Antwerp by the name of Faszczak. Maybe
you would like to meet him and his family," and he gave us
their phone number. We were so busy with the store, we never
called. Now we had plenty of time. We went over to their table
and I said, "My name is Miedzianagora; my brother is. . . ." I
didn't need to say anything more. They both jumped up from

their chairs and gave me and Betty big hugs. "Of course, we know who you are! Our niece Jagda is married to your brother Jakob. We are *michpuchah* [family]." So we sat down with them and we were talking all evening. They were very nice people, much older than us — I was thirty-nine at that time and Betty was thirty-one. We made a date to meet them again the next afternoon at the same café. This time, we came with our whole family and they brought their two sons, their daughter, and their granddaughter with them.

After that we were seeing the Faszczaks almost every day. We would meet in the afternoon around four o'clock at the same café where we met them the first time. Always we were talking about the military-political situation and agreeing that it was getting very bad and we should try to get out of Europe — go to Spain and try to get visas to North or South America. Or if we couldn't get visas from Spain, maybe we could get into Portugal or Morocco and get visas from there. But it was almost impossible now to get into Spain. Franco was not letting in refugees. We were hoping maybe he would change his mind soon, but weeks went by and nothing changed. One day we were sitting at the café with the Faszczaks and their two sons, when Maurice, the younger brother said, "If we can't get into Spain legally, let's try to get in illegally. We'll find a smuggler to take us over the Pyrénées mountains by foot, and get us counterfeit Spanish *cartes de séjour.* We've talked about this before, but now it's time to stop talking and do it."

"It's a nice idea," I said, "but tell me, how am I going to get my mother with her heart condition, my sister Fella who is so tired after she has walked for twenty minutes that she has to take a twenty-minute rest, and my three-year-old daughter to climb through the Pyrénées?"

"We couldn't do it either," the older Monsieur Faszczak said. He was pointing to his wife and himself. "We are too old."

"And our little Hélène is too young," Madame Faszczak said. She was talking about her granddaughter who was maybe two years old.

Chana Faszczak in Poland with her niece Jagda, mid 1930s

Usually Betty had plenty to say, but now she was sitting very quiet. Probably she was scared to say what she was thinking, but after a while she said, "Listen, we are mostly worried that if the Germans take over Southern France, they will take the Jewish men prisoners, or maybe even kill them. They are not going to hurt women and children. Maybe I should take the children, your mother, Fella, and Rifke and drive back to Brussels. And you Henyek can go with Maurice and Jules into Spain through the mountains. I haven't gotten any news from my father and brother since we left La Panne. At least I'll find out how they are."

"I think she is right," Monsieur Faszczak said. "The Germans are not going to be interested in an old man like me either. Maybe Chana and I, and Bella and Hélène, should stay here in Gaillac for a while; maybe go back to Belgium later on. Then Henyek, Maurice, and Jules can get into Spain and they won't have to worry about us."

"This is a very big decision," Madame Faszczak said. "We have to think about it, and wait at least another week or so to see if maybe Spain will let us in."

We waited a week, but nothing changed. So the two Faszczak sons and I decided we would try to get into Spain together, and Betty was going to drive back to Belgium. How could we know that the Nazis would murder babies, that they would gas women and children, and old people?

Once we decided, we didn't wait long. We got *laissez-passer* [transit permits] to go to Toulouse. There were so many refugees by this time that there were barricades on the roads and you had to have a permit to go from one town to another. A few days later, I gave Betty a lot of money — I had a belt with a zipper and I was always keeping the money — and she drove me in the morning to take the bus to Toulouse.

We were sitting in a café at the bus stop waiting for the Faszczak boys. When they arrived, I was very surprised to see that Jules was carrying a suitcase. "What are you doing with that suitcase?" I asked him. "If we are going to climb through the Pyrénées mountains, we are going to need backpacks, not suitcases."

"That's exactly what I told him, but he wouldn't listen to me," Maurice said. Madame Faszczak and Betty agreed with us. Now Jules had four people telling him to get a backpack.

"*Jullie hebben gewonnen* [You have won]," Jules said, and threw up his arms. A lot of times, the Faszczaks were mixing in some Flemish — this is what they speak in Antwerp.

So the brothers and I went to a luggage store close by to exchange the suitcase for a backpack. Jules picked one out and paid for it. We had plenty of time until the next bus, so we were standing in the store schmoozing with the owner. "You have come a long way from Belgium," he said.

"How do you know we are from Belgium?" I asked him. This was a joke. As soon as you open your mouth, French people recognize the Belgian accent.

We laughed, and then we told him our stories. After a while, he asked, "Do you have somewhere to stay in Toulouse?" We said "no," so he took out a piece of paper and he wrote something down. He gave it to us and said, "This is my address in Toulouse; you can stay this night with me — I have a big apartment." I had already noticed that in general, just like the weather, the people in Southern France were warmer than in the North. We shook hands with Monsieur Leclair, and thanked him a thousand times.

In the meantime, Betty was sitting with Madame Faszczak in the café at the bus stop. "What took you so long?" they both asked when we got back.

"We were talking to the store owner," I said. "What a nice guy! He told us we could stay in his apartment in Toulouse tonight." I took out from my pocket the piece of paper with his address and showed it to Betty. It's a very good thing she wrote down the address. Pretty soon, the next bus came. We said "good-bye," and we were all crying.

All her life Betty has talked about what Madame Faszczak said to her after the bus left: "Madame Miedzianagora, I am getting a very bad feeling; I don't think we are doing the right thing. We didn't even try to get into Spain; maybe we could get in together. You are very young; you don't remember World War I, but I do — if you separated from your family the war went by and you didn't see them again. I don't think we have tried hard enough to stay together. I might not even be able to get a letter from my sons and you from your husband for the entire war. I am afraid we have made a terrible mistake." When Betty heard these words, she knew that she was right. Those few words changed our lives. Betty and the children would not be alive if Madame Faszczak had not said them.

A lot of people would think, "Maybe she is right, but how can I be sure? I need time to think it over; I can't just change my mind so fast." Betty is not like this. Once she gets an idea and she thinks it's a good idea, she doesn't wait. She doesn't ask for other people's opinions; she acts right away. So she went straight back to our apartment and repeated to my mother and Fella and Rifke what Madame Faszczak said. "So I have changed my mind. I am taking the children to Toulouse right away to be with Henyek and we will at least try to get into Spain together," she told them. "Fella was very upset," Betty told me later, "but your mother agreed with me and said, 'You are absolutely right. You shouldn't separate from your husband.'"

So my mother, Fella, and Rifke stayed in Gaillac. Betty gave them most of the money I had left her.

18

BETTY HAS TOLD SO many times the story of how she made it to Toulouse without a *laissez-passer* and even got there before I did, I know every detail. After she said good-bye to my mother, Fella, and Rifke, she put the children in the car and drove to the Faszczaks' apartment — they lived not far away. Madame Faszczak had asked her to do this. She told her, "I will go home and talk to my husband and daughter; I think they will agree with me. So please, before you leave for Toulouse, stop at our house and if they have said "yes," we can all go together — we will follow you in our car." And this is what happened. When Betty got to the Faszczaks, they were already bringing down their suitcase.

It was very easy to pack in those days because we refugees had next to nothing — a change of clothes, some underwear, a toothbrush. In one of the towns where we stayed overnight, Betty had bought herself a dark blue dress with a lot of little flowers in many different colors. "I can wear this for weeks and it won't show the dirt," she told me and she was right. She was wearing this dress almost all the time. Sometimes at night, if we were staying in a hotel, she would wash it a little under the arms because she was sweating so much and it was smelling bad. Even if it was still a little wet under the arms, she would put it on in the morning. It didn't matter because in a few hours it was wet from sweat again.

So now, Madame Faszczak, her husband, her daughter, and granddaughter got into their car and they followed Betty. Outside of Gaillac there was a barricade with gendarmes who asked for a *laissez-passer*. Betty told them, "I am a Polish citizen; my husband is a diplomat, and is already in Toulouse. The Polish consul in Toulouse is waiting for us. He has a plane ready to take us to London and I don't have a *laissez-passer* because there was no time." In every little town where they were stopped, she told the same story and each time they said, "*Passez.*" When she was finished telling the story, she pointed to the Faszczaks' car and said, "Those people are also Polish and they are with me."

While they were driving to Toulouse by car, Maurice, Jules, and I were on a bus that was stopping in every little town, and after we got to Toulouse, we had to take a bus to get to Monsieur Leclair's apartment. Finally, we got off the bus and found his street. We started looking for the house with the right number, when all of a sudden far down the street, I see two children who look like Joe and Myriam running towards me so fast and yelling, "Papi, papi, papi." I thought I was dreaming. How can this be my children? They are in Gaillac, or already on their way back to Brussels. But then they came closer, and Myriam grabbed my leg, and Joe hugged me by the waist. I saw Betty. She was locking the doors to the car and then she started to walk towards me. For a few seconds, I couldn't say a word.

When Betty came close to us, Maurice, Jules, and I all asked her at the same time, "What happened? What are you doing here? Why are you in Toulouse?"

Betty said to the boys, "Listen, it isn't only me; your parents, Bella, and Hélène are here too. We decided that it was a big mistake to separate and that we should try to get into Spain together. We were all very thirsty so they went to get a few bottles of mineral water. They will be here any minute."

We were angry. "What is wrong with you?" we asked. "We made a decision together what is the best thing to do. How will we be able to get into Spain with little children? We will all be stuck here in Southern France."

"We made a decision, but it was the wrong decision. After you got on the bus, Madame Faszczak realized what a mistake we made." And then Betty told us exactly what Madame Faszczak had said to her.

When I was sitting on the bus to Toulouse, I was looking out the window and thinking, "When will I see my family again? It could be years. At least Joe will recognize me, but Myriam is so little, she might not even remember me," and I was trying not to cry. Now I was holding Myriam and she had her little arms around my neck. Joe was holding me tight by the waist. I decided maybe Madame Faszczak was right. Even if I had to carry Myriam all the way over the Pyrénées — I was very strong in those days — at least we would be together.

Betty and I knew that to have any chance of getting into Spain legally, we had to go to the Polish consulate in Toulouse and get passports. We had applied for Belgian citizenship a few years before — it was very hard for foreign-born residents to become citizens — and in the beginning of May they had told us that everything was in order and in a few months we would be Belgian citizens. If only we had those Belgian passports, everything would have been so easy!

Because we were very sure that we would get Belgian citizenship, we did not even bother to renew our Polish passports. Well, the truth is we did go to the Polish consulate in Brussels to renew our passports, but the official at the consulate got very mad at Betty because she started to laugh when he said something to her in Polish. She knew about five Polish words, mostly bad words.

"*Panye* Miedzianagora, why do you laugh when I speak to you in Polish? You should be studying our language not laughing at it," he said to her. He had a terrible accent when he spoke French.

And then he looked at me and said in Polish, "You should be teaching Polish, and respect for our country, to your wife." I translated what he said for Betty. She tried not to laugh again, but just from looking at her face — she was rolling her eyes — he could see what she was thinking.

Because her father was a Polish citizen, Betty had been a Polish citizen all her life — even her German mother had to become Polish when she married Abraham. Always it was the husband's nationality that counted. Betty had been in Poland that one time when she went to visit my family, and she thought it was absurd that she was the citizen of a country that she had nothing to do with, didn't understand the language, and had spent four weeks there. The idea that she should learn Polish was especially ridiculous.

So this guy threw us out of the consulate. "Come back when your wife no longer laughs at our language and our country," he told me — in Polish.

Betty was still laughing when we got out of the building, "Who cares about a Polish passport; soon we will be good Belgian citizens," and she raised her arm and yelled, "*Vive la Belgique* [Long live Belgium]!"

I was angry. "You should not have laughed like that," I told her, "It was very embarrassing and now we don't have any passports." But I thought too that we would soon have our Belgian passports and so I didn't think it was such a big deal.

Now we needed those Polish passports urgently. The morning after we arrived in Toulouse, we got the address of the Polish consulate. Betty found an iron and ironed my shirt, my suit pants, and her flower dress — this was the only time in my life I saw her lift an iron. I shined our shoes. We got dressed, left the children with the Faszczaks, and took a bus to go to the consulate. It was a pretty long bus ride and Betty asked me to write down how you say in Polish, "Good morning," "I am Madame Miedzianagora," "I like Poland very much," "I am sorry that I do not speak more Polish," and other stuff like this. I wrote everything down phonetically and she was repeating "*dzien dobry,*" "*bardzo lubie Polske,*" "*Przykro mi, ze nie mowie wiecej po polsku . . .*" over and over until we got off the bus.

By the time we walked into the consulate building, she had learned maybe twenty new Polish words, but she didn't get a chance to impress the consul. We followed the signs to the office and soon we were stopped by a couple of boy scouts standing in the hallway. They were talking to each other and laughing, but as soon as they saw us, they stood up straight, like soldiers. Betty and I looked at each other — what are boy scouts doing here?

"*Bonjour,*" I said, "we are here to see the consul."

"The consulate is closed indefinitely. The consul has fled from Toulouse; he went to London."

"But we are Polish citizens and we need passports urgently," I told them.

"There are plenty of passports in the office, but we have no right to let you or anyone in."

"But *pan* Kowalski is an old friend of mine from Poland," I told them. "He was expecting us. He must have left very suddenly. Isn't there someone else who could help us?" (I had read the name of the consul — Roman Kowalski — on the plaque near the front door to the building.)

"No, there is no one from the consulate here, just us; we were asked to help out to make sure no one gets in. We cannot make exceptions."

This was a very bad situation. While we were talking to them and thinking what to do, another couple came over. These people were very angry when they found out that the consul had run away. They were yelling very loud at the boy scouts and swearing in Polish, "*niech to szlag trafi* [damn it]" and other stuff like this. So while this was going on, we walked very quietly down the hall. We got to the door of the consul's office and the boys were still so busy with the other people, they didn't see what we were doing. I tried to turn the door-knob and I couldn't believe how lucky we were — the door was not locked. Probably the consul left in such a hurry he forgot to lock it. We went into the office.

"The boys will think that we left the building," Betty whispered to me.

"Yes, but how will we get out of the building?"

"Let's find some passports first, then we'll worry about getting out."

It was daytime, so we didn't have to turn on any lights. Very, very quietly we opened drawers and pretty soon we found blank passports. We took two and I filled them out. We had brought pictures. I found some glue and we attached them. We looked around some more and found the official Polish government stamp. I stamped the passports. While I was doing some of this, Betty was looking around the room to see if there was any other way to get out.

When I was finished, she said, "Listen, we could jump out the window, but it's concrete outside and the ground floor is pretty high on this side of the building."

"Do we have a choice?" I asked.

"I noticed when we were sneaking down the hall that the hallway continues to the left just a little bit after the entrance to this office. If we can make it to there and turn the corner, the boy scouts won't be able to see us and maybe we can find another way out of the building."

"What if they do see us?"

"Give me the passports. I'll put them inside my girdle."

"That's a very good idea. If they stop us, I'll tell them that my good friend Roman was always writing to me about what a beautiful office he has, so I wanted to take a look at it. See those big oil paintings on the wall — the Polish countryside, portraits of Pilsudski and other big shots. See that big Persian rug on the floor. Roman was telling me about all these things in his letters!"

"Very good," Betty said. "Between your talent for telling stories and my girdle, I think we will be fine. What are they going to do? Ask to look in my girdle? They'll look in my pocketbook and in our clothes pockets and that's all."

I agreed with her. "If the police cared very much about what is happening at the Polish consulate, they would not have sent a couple of sixteen-year-old boy scouts to guard the place."

"Exactly. Let's wait until the boys are busy with new people, and then try to get out."

And this is what we did. We stood next to the door and listened — we left it just a tiny bit open. First we just heard the boys talking and laughing; one of them was imitating a Polish accent. It took maybe ten minutes until we heard people talking to the boys. Everybody was upset when they found out that the consul was gone, so they were talking very loud, complaining. Very quietly, we walked out of the office away from them. It helped us that the boy scouts were always facing the other direction — from where new people were coming.

We found a back entrance that was locked from the outside, but not from the inside. So we left the building with two shiny new passports in Betty's girdle. We were officially Polish citizens again. Everything had happened so fast. It was like having a very bad dream and then all of a sudden you wake up and everything is okay again.

We walked down the street and went into the first café we could find. Betty went downstairs to the W.C. and took out the passports and put them in her pocketbook. "I am sweating so much, the covers were wet," she told me when she came back to the table, "but I wiped them off with my handkerchief and now they have a nice leather smell." She took the two passports out to show me. First I smelled them, then I kissed them, and then I gave them back to Betty to put in her pocketbook.

So now we were ready to go to Perpignan, a town very close to the Spanish border. This is where you could try to get transit visas through Spain and visas to Morocco or Portugal.

19

THE NEXT MORNING WE said good-bye to the Faszczaks. We put the children and our suitcase in the car and started driving. When we got close to Perpignan there was a barricade. This was not a little barricade with a few French soldiers like we saw before. Here were Senegalese soldiers on horses with bayonets aimed at us. Right away I said to Betty, "This does not look good." A French officer came over to the car. He didn't even say "*bonjour*," only one word, "*laissez-passer.*" Betty told him that we were Polish diplomats and the Polish consul in Barcelona was waiting for us to fly us to London. He stood there while she was talking and not one muscle on his face moved. His body was like a block of wood. The second she finished, he said without any change in his expression, "*demi-tour* [about turn]." We looked at him and we looked at the bayonets and we knew that we could not bluff our way through this time.

So we made a *demi-tour*. We drove a few minutes and then I saw a bench on the side of the road. "Stop the car," I told Betty. "Let's sit down on that bench and we will try to figure out how we can get into Perpignan."

As soon as we got out of the car, the children started complaining. "It's too hot, I don't like it here," Myriam was saying. For weeks already she was saying all the time, "It's too hot." She was used to nice, cool Belgian weather. She didn't know yet that soon it was going to get much more hot.

"Why can't we go back in the car and drive? You can talk in the car," Joe said. At least in the car, they had some shade and a breeze. Here we were sitting in maybe ninety-five-degree Fahrenheit heat in the middle of the day, baking in the sun.

"We can't waste gasoline," Betty told him.

"Why can't we at least find a shady place to sit?"

Just as he said this, a farmer walked by and heard him. He looked at Joe and said, "*Ah oui, mon petit, il fait bien chaud aujourdhui* [Oh yes, my little one, it is very hot today]."

Right away Betty and I said "hello" and started talking with him. We told him what happened at the barricade, and asked, "Is there some other way to get to Perpignan?"

He said, "Yes, but it's very complicated and difficult; you have to go maybe 150 kilometers out of the way in a circular route through the French Pyrénées mountains, very close to the Spanish border, then you will come into Perpignan from the side of town that is close to Spain. There are no refugees trying to get in from that side, so there will be no barricades."

Betty was holding the map in her hand. "Can you show us this route on the map?" she asked.

I took out a pen and gave it to him and he underlined on the map which roads to take, but once he got to the Pyrénées, there was nothing to underline. He made a zigzag line through the mountains.

"As you can see, the road that I am telling you about does not even appear on the map. Very little of it is paved and it is very narrow."

We were standing next to a field with cows. He pointed to them and said, "The road is mostly for them and for the goats. It will not be easy to drive on it."

"We don't have a choice," Betty said.

We thanked him. He wished us good luck and started to walk away. I had noticed that Myriam was staring at him all the time while he was talking; she even stopped complaining about the heat. He had just taken a few steps when she said, "How come that man talks sooo funny?" We all went "sshh" and then Joe said in a low voice, "The people in the *Midi* have a different accent, not everyone talks the way we do in Belgium. Didn't you notice that before?"

"I did notice," Myriam said. "But this man talks even funnier."

"He talks exactly the way they talk in *Marius, Fanny, et César*," Betty said.

This was a famous movie trilogy about some poor people in Marseilles. When we were first married, Betty wanted very much that I should go with her to see *Marius,* but I said, "You know I don't like movies." She tried to get me to change my mind, but still I said "no," and she was angry at me. (I never changed. In my whole life, I went to maybe five or six movies. It's always the same — boring love stories or people killing each other. I have seen enough killing in my life; I don't need to pay money to see more in a movie theater.) So she called up Frieda and they went together and saw all three films. Frieda was Betty's cousin and they were friends since they were children in Germany. They were crazy about these movies; even years later they were talking about them.

"Listen, we have to go through the mountains the way he told us," Betty said, "What else are we going to do? Sit here and wait for the Senegalese with their bayonets and the French Nazi to go away?"

I knew she was right, but it has always made me very scared to drive on roads high in the mountains. Once when Joe was still a baby we went on a vacation in the Ardennes mountains. We were driving on a very narrow twisting road. It made me so nervous when I looked out the window that I started to sweat and I had to close my eyes until we got lower down. The Pyrénées mountains are much higher than the Ardennes. I started to say, "Maybe we should wait, . . . " but then I changed in the middle and said, "Yes, we have to do it. There is no other way."

So we got in the car and started driving first west and then south. Like the farmer said, going through the Pyrénées was very slow. We were on dirt roads and sometimes we had to sit and wait while cows or goats were crossing. A few times a farmer in a truck was coming in the opposite direction and we had to back up. When this happened, I was so scared when I looked down the mountain I thought I would have a heart attack.

We stopped overnight in two small mountain towns. In those days you had to register at the police headquarters or at the mayor's office. In one town, when we told the mayor our Polish consul story, he said, "I know you are lying, but it's okay, I understand."

When we got out of his office, Betty said, "He is not the only one. We will never know how many of the French gendarmes really believed our story about the Polish consul, and how many wanted to help refugees get away from the Nazis."

"Even if they didn't believe us, still we gave them a reason to let us through."

In Gaillac, Betty had bought a hat to keep out the sun. In later years in Los Angeles, we got used to the very bright light, but in those days we had never been so far south and it was difficult to get used to the Mediterranean sun. The second morning in the Pyrénées, the car window was open and all of a sudden Betty's hat flew out and dropped a few thousand feet down the mountain. The children got very excited. Joe was sitting by the window behind Betty and he was looking out and saying, "I can see it! I can see your hat. It's flying around; the wind is blowing it back and forth." He was disappointed when he couldn't see it anymore. Myriam was upset because she couldn't see the hat flying around, and then she was asking, "Aren't we going to go and look for *mamy*'s hat?" Joe was shaking his head and making a face like older children make when the little one is saying something very silly and they feel so smart.

I was thinking, "Better the hat should drop than the car." One little mistake and we were finished.

Betty said, "I don't like to wear hats anyway."

20

THE THIRD DAY, WE got to Perpignan from the Spanish side and there were no Senegalese, no bayonets, no French Nazis, no barricades. We drove right into town. It was around the middle or end of July. More than two months had gone by since we left Brussels. We were following the signs to the center of town, and pretty soon we got to a nice little square with trees and lots of stores and cafés and people. All of a sudden Joe starts yelling, "Look! Look! There's Bernhardt!" Bernhardt was Betty's cousin — Frieda's brother. We all started to yell, "Bernhardt! Bernhardt!" He heard us and turned around and was looking and looking. Maybe it was harder for him to see us because he was blind in one eye. Finally, he got a big smile on his face and he was waving back. Betty parked the car and we all got out and were hugging and kissing. We were so happy to see family; we had no idea that Bernhardt had even left Brussels.

One of the first things he told us was, "They have started to give out visas to Morocco at the local government office, and the Spanish government is now giving transit visas to Spain."

It was like a miracle. We wouldn't have to find a smuggler to take us through the Pyrénées and get us counterfeit Spanish residence cards. We could just drive into Spain.

Bernhardt got in the car with us. "Now we can all go to lunch. I'm so hungry," Joe said. "I'm hungry, too," Myriam said.

"I will take you to a nice restaurant, but first I will take you to register at the *lycée* [high school] where there are cots for the refugees," Bernhardt said. "You will need a place to sleep tonight."

"Can't we just get a *beignet* or a croissant or something like that?" Joe said.

He said this at the right moment. Betty pulled over to the curb. We were in front of a bakery.

"Henyek, get the children a baguette. We can all have a few bites. I am hungry, too."

So I ran in and got a baguette and the children became quiet. We went to the school and signed up for four cots. Then Bernhardt took us to a small restaurant near the square where Joe first saw him.

After we sat down and ordered, he told us, "I think I will go back to Belgium." His wife and little boy Raymond were in Brussels. "I just got a letter from home — the Germans are not bothering anybody, not even the young men. Life goes on as usual."

This is how a lot of people got tricked — the Gestapo didn't start to round up Jews and send them to concentration camps until 1942, so Bernhardt and many others went back. It was a terrible mistake.

The government offices were already closed that day, so the next morning I went to get visas to Morocco. Bernhardt came with me. A few hundred people were waiting in line outside the building. We got behind them and were waiting almost an hour, and the line moved maybe six feet. So I said, "Bernhardt, stay here. I will come right back; I want to see something." I left the line and took a walk around the building — on one side was an empty lot. The line was in the other direction. I saw that the visa office had a window in the back and it was open. I went back to Bernhardt and I said very loud, "I am tired of waiting in this line; let's come back tomorrow."

He looked at me like I was crazy. "But it will be just as bad tomorrow," he said.

I pulled him by the arm and from the look on my face he could tell that I had a plan. I took him in the direction of the empty lot and told him, "By the time we would have gotten to the office, they may already have given out all the visas. I just saw that the back window to the visa office is open. Come with me — you can help me up and I will climb in."

"*Henyek, bist du verrueckt* [Are you crazy]?" Bernhardt grew up in Germany just like Betty, so he was mixing in some German — especially when he was upset or excited — with the French. "They will throw you right out."

"Don't worry; I will take care of it — and I showed him my wallet."

So we went to the back of the building. Bernhardt gave me a push and I climbed inside the office. A man was standing right near the window and saw me. He started yelling — "What are you doing here? Get out!" So, right away, I pulled out some francs, and I said, "*Monsieur,* I have small sick children, I am desperate. Please help me," and I gave him a nice amount of money. After about ten, fifteen minutes, he brought me visas.

"You can't go out through the front, the people in line will kill you," the man told me. He showed me another exit from the back of the building.

I went out and right away I saw Bernhardt waiting for me not far from the window that I had climbed in.

"*Fait accompli,*" I told him. "The Moroccan visas are in my pocket. Let's go have a coffee, and then I will go to get Spanish transit visas."

The line was not so long to get the Spanish visas. I didn't have to climb through windows; I didn't have to give a *schmeer.* When I met Betty and the children — we had made a rendezvous to meet late in the afternoon at a café — I had in my hands everything we needed to get out of France and into Spain and Morocco. We could have gotten in the car and right away gone to the border, but we got suspicious.

When I came to the café, Betty was sitting with Bernhardt and maybe six or seven other refugees — wherever we went, the refugees always found a café where they were getting together every day.

Everybody was asking the same questions: "Why have they made it so easy for us to go to Morocco? Maybe it's a trick. Maybe Hitler's going to take over Morocco and that's why they're letting us go there. And why is Franco suddenly giving out so many visas? Maybe he made a deal with Hitler that they'll put us in camps in Spain or send us back." Most of the people in the café already had visas and transit visas, but they were still in Perpignan because they were worried.

By the time Betty and I left the café, we were worried, too. "Maybe they are right; maybe it's a trick," I said.

Betty said, "Listen, before you came to the café, there was a couple from Czechoslovakia at our table — he is a doctor — and they read in a magazine that Franco is a Marrano and that is why he wants to help Jews. I have read that Mohammed, the King of Morocco, is very friendly to Jews."

Betty was less suspicious than me, but still she was worried. "But it is also true," she continued, "that the Vichy French control Morocco and Franco is friends with Hitler."

"Maybe we should wait a few days before going to Spain; maybe we can find out a little more what is really going on."

She agreed and we waited. But after a few days the situation was not getting any better. The Germans were in control of half of France; they had started bombing England. So we decided to take a chance. We said good-bye to Bernhardt, and he told us he was going back to Belgium the next day. This was the last time we saw him. The Nazis killed him and his wife. At least his little boy Raymond survived.

◆ ◆ ◆

We got in the car and drove to a little border town called Le Perthus in the middle of the Pyrénées mountains — very beautiful, but we did not enjoy it.

We got to the frontier around one in the afternoon. A French gendarme stopped us and asked, "Where are you going?" Betty took our Spanish transit visas out of her handbag and showed them to him.

"*Pauvres malheureux,*" he lamented. "The Spanish just closed the border two hours ago."

So many refugees were going into Spain that the government decided to close the border even to people who had visas. Such bad luck we had — two hours earlier they would have let us across.

The frontier was on a long narrow street called l'Avenue de France that was running through the whole town. One half of the street (and the town) was in Spain and the other half in France. So now we turned around and parked the car in the French section. We went into every café and store to ask if anybody knew a place for us to sleep. Some of the people didn't even speak French, or very little. They were Catalan. They all said "no."

We were getting very hungry, so we bought some bread and a few tomatoes and we went to a park and sat down on a bench and ate. After we ate, we put Myriam in the back of the car to take a nap. By the time she woke up, it was already early in the evening, and we had no place to sleep. We were thinking maybe we will have to sleep in the car.

We were all very thirsty, so we went back to a café in town and sat down outside to drink something. We were sitting there maybe a half-hour, when we saw an old lady walking down the street. She was a widow dressed in black and she had a very bad limp. Betty said, "We have nothing to lose; I'm going to ask her," and she jumped up to talk to the woman.

"Yes, I have a room I can rent you," she told Betty. "Come with me."

The room was the size of a king-size bed. At night, Betty and the children slept and I sat with a shoe in my hand and killed the cockroaches and ants and other bugs. The second or third day we were there, Myriam got sick with German measles. She had a fever and a pink rash all over her body, so we put her to bed, but she got up, and she started to jump up and down on the bed. She was tearing her nightshirt and screaming over and over again, "I want to go home, I want to go home, I want my bed, I want my bed." There were no doctors in this town, but the doctor from Czechoslovakia that Betty met in the café in Perpignan was also stuck with his wife and daughter in Le Perthus. They had run away from Prague a few years before and were living in France, and they also wanted to get to Spain. He was a very nice man. I went to get him — their room was about the same size as ours — and he came with me to examine Myriam. He did whatever he could. I don't think we could even get any medicine in this town.

For a couple of days we were eating bread and tomatoes. Later on, we started to get a little more food. A few doors away from where we were staying was a little grocery store where Betty was shopping.

One day, she bought a can of soup and she asked the owner, "Would you be kind enough to warm it up for me? I have a sick child and nothing warm to give her." The woman lived right in back of the store, and Betty could see the stove from the store.

But she said, "No. When our Spanish children were starving on the border the French didn't let them in. Your child is not starving. Why should I be kind to you? Why should I warm up your soup?" A lot of Catalan were very angry at French people. Because we were speaking French, they hated us.

During the Spanish Civil War, which had just ended a year before, hundreds of thousands of Spanish people had tried to escape into France, and for some time the French didn't let them in. Hundreds of Spanish refugees died on the Spanish side of town. Finally, the French did let them in and they even set up a temporary hospital in the Fort de Bellegarde for the wounded soldiers from the Republican army. But many Spanish refugees had no place to stay; they were camping out on the streets, so the Catalan people did not feel sorry for us. We had a room to sleep in and something to eat.

But not everyone was like the woman in the grocery store. One day Betty met a Catalan lady who was also shopping there. They started talking and Betty told her how sick Myriam was and she had nothing warm to feed her, and this lady let Betty use her kitchen to warm up some food.

Every morning we would go to the Spanish guards and ask them when the border would be opened and every morning they said "*mañana, mañana* [tomorrow, tomorrow]."

After two weeks they opened the border, but Myriam was still very sick. We asked the doctor, "What are we going to do?" He said, "As a doctor I have to tell you that you should not move the child. As a refugee, I say let's take her in the car and I will go with you." So we took him and his family with us and we drove to Barcelona.

21

WE HAD TO BE very careful with our money. There was no way to get any more from the bank in Brussels or New York and we had no idea how long we would be refugees. But after two weeks in that tiny dirty room and two months sleeping in barns and schools, we decided to stay one night at the Ritz Hotel in Barcelona. I was so tired from staying up all night fighting with cockroaches and ants, my dream was to sleep at least one night in a big comfortable bed with clean pillows and sheets. We walked into the hotel sweating, dirty, in wrinkled clothes that had not been washed in weeks, but we had the money and they rented us a room.

I still remember that hotel like it was yesterday. When you walked into the lobby, on the right, was the door to the dining room. The tables were covered with white tablecloths and cloth napkins and lots of different forks and knives and spoons and beautiful crystal glasses. Big windows with pulled-back, thick, wine-colored velvet drapes looked out on the boulevard filled with trees. When the bellhop opened the door to our room we thought we were looking at a palace. A thick dark-green carpet, a beautiful wood-carved headboard on our bed, fresh flowers in a crystal vase. We even had our own private bathroom. We all took baths and Betty washed out some clothes — it was very hot, so everything dried fast. We had left Brussels with an overnight bag, so we had to buy a few things on the way, but we didn't have much more than one change of clothes.

Myriam started to feel better in Barcelona. When we first came into the city, we were driving near the Mediterranean and she got very excited, "Look! Look! What a big ocean!" In Belgium, she loved very much going to the beach; she never wanted to get out of the water. We used to call her "the little herring." In this she is taking after Betty — whenever they see water, right away they want to jump in. In Barcelona at least she got to take a bath in our beautiful bathroom.

Madrid was about 400 kilometers from Barcelona and this was our next stop. It was soon after the Civil War, and Spain was so poor. One time, we stopped in a town — Betty went into a grocery store to buy something cold to drink — the children and I were sitting in the car eating bananas. We threw some peel into the gutter and a man came up and started talking to me in Spanish. I couldn't understand what he was saying; he kept repeating the word "*platano*." Finally he bent down and picked up our banana peels and he pointed a finger to the peel and then to his mouth. He was so hungry he was asking me if he could take the banana peel and eat it! I told him "*si*" and I gave him a few pesos.

When we got to Madrid, we found a small hotel, not expensive but clean. The owner and his family had an apartment in the hotel. *Señor* Marquez told us that one of his grandmothers was from Perpignan and this is why he was speaking such good French. He was a good-looking, tall man about my age with curly light brown hair, a little mustache, and blue eyes. *Señor* Marquez had only one arm. We thought probably he lost the other one in the Civil War.

He looked at Myriam and Joe and said, "What beautiful children you have!" And then he told us, "I have a sixteen-year-old daughter, Consuela. She is going to high school and studying French, so if you need someone to look after them, she would be very happy to have an opportunity to practice French. It is summertime, so she is on vacation."

Our first day in Madrid, Betty and I sat down and made a list of all the countries in North, South, and Central America and we divided up the list. She would go to half the consulates or embassies and I would go to the other half to ask for visas. We hired Consuela to stay with the children.

Right away, Betty went to the American Embassy — this was our first choice. They told her that the quota list was so long that it would take ten to fifteen years before we could get to the United States. She came back to the hotel very disappointed. So then we started going down the rest of the list — Canada, Chili, Argentina, Uruguay, and on and on. Every one of them said the same thing — "no." We were getting more and more worried.

When I walked out of the Brazilian consulate, I was ready to cry. I was standing waiting for the elevator, and next to me was an older man with grey hair and a thick mustache. I could see he was wearing a very expensive suit, not like mine. He was looking at me — it was taking a long time for the elevator to come — and finally he said something in Spanish. I answered in French, "I am sorry. I do not speak Spanish,"

"But I speak French," he answered. "You look very upset. Perhaps I can help you." He had a very good accent in French. The man was a Spanish Jew who lived in Madrid. This was very unusual. In 1492, they gave the Spanish Jews a choice — either you become Catholic or we kill you. So a lot of Spanish Catholics have Jewish ancestors, but Jews living in Spain....I had never heard of such a thing.

So I told this man our story and he said, "I am a good friend of the consul; we just had lunch together. Let me go in and talk to him."

A few minutes later he came out with the consul. The Jewish man was tall and thin with a head full of curly hair, the consul was short and fat and bald; they looked funny next to each other. The consul invited me into his office. As soon as I looked at his desk, I saw that it was almost exactly the same as my desk in my office on Avenue Coghen. It was made of cherrywood. The sides and the front were carved into squares with a molded border around each square.

I was so busy running from Hitler, I didn't have a lot of time to think about home, but when I saw this desk I remembered that I once lived in a twelve-room apartment with beautiful furniture, and a big terrace with stairs leading to a garden with apple and pear trees and bushes with gooseberries and red currants. My wife and I went to work every day, but always came home for a few hours for lunch with our family. On Sundays if the weather was nice, we took the children to the *Bois de la Cambre*. In the woods was a nice ice-skating rink and Betty liked a lot to ice skate. She was teaching Joe. I was sitting with Myriam in the café around the rink. For me, I would order a cup of tea or coffee and an apple tart, for Myriam a hot chocolate, and a *Merveilleux*. (In Belgium and France each little pastry has a different name.) This was her favorite — meringue with whipped cream and chocolate cream, and little chocolate sprinkles all around the outside. Most of the time we would meet friends at the café. If it was raining or cold, family and friends came to our apartment and we played cards.

Now I was a beggar asking people over and over, "Please, please take me in." And so far the answer was always "no."

The consul spoke a very nice French but with a strong accent. Right away he was asking me a lot of questions. "What is your citizenship? What is your work? How big is your family? Are you all in good health? How much money do you have?"

I answered everything, and when I told him that I had a couple of thousand dollars with me, but also I had ten thousand dollars at the First National City Bank in New York, his eyes opened up very big.

He said, "Of course, we will have to wire the bank in New York, but once we receive confirmation then there will be no problem getting visas for you and your family. It will probably take about ten days to two weeks."

"But our permit to stay in Spain is only for another seventy-two hours," I told him. "Is it maybe possible to get the visa faster?"

"No, I cannot do anything about this," he said. "After we hear back from your bank, we have to wire Rio to get the official permit and then we have a lot of paperwork to take care of. Why don't you try to get an extension of your permit?"

"I will try," I said and I thanked them both — the Jewish guy was sitting with us the whole time.

I went back to the hotel feeling a little better. I told Betty what happened and we decided that we would go together to the government office to extend our residence permit for another two weeks.

The next morning, we were waiting in line to speak to an official and right in front of us was a German woman with blonde hair in a braid on top of her head. When she turned around, we could see she was wearing a necklace with a big swastika on it. When she got to the desk of the Spanish official, she handed him her passport. He looked at it and gave her a big smile. Then they were talking for a long time, very friendly. We got scared when we saw this.

When she was finished, we went up and showed him our Polish passports and told him we needed an extension of our residence permit. We explained about the visa to Brazil and the guy shook his head — "no." We asked him a second time and he said "no." We tried one more time — we could see that he was getting very angry — and again he said "no." We decided not to argue anymore with him because we were afraid that this Spanish Nazi could have us arrested. So we walked out feeling like somebody spit in our face. Without a residence permit, we could not stay in Spain.

Consuela told us that she could only babysit for a few hours that day, so we decided to take a taxi back to the hotel. The driver was a very friendly guy and he spoke some French. We were talking and after a while we told him our story.

He said, "I am a communist — I hate those fascist pigs, Franco and Hitler. I would like to help you. I have an extra bedroom in my apartment — my little girl is spending a few weeks with her grandmother in Seville — and if you want you can stay with us until you get the visas for Brazil. The bed is big enough for two people and we could put some blankets down on the floor for your children to sleep."

This was a dangerous thing to do, for him and for us. He gave us his name and address and we told him that we had to think about it. If we decided to stay with him, we would come over to his apartment the next evening at eight o'clock. He didn't have a telephone. When I paid for the taxi ride, I tried to give him a nice amount of extra pesos — whether we stayed at his house or not, he was offering to take a big risk to help us — but he didn't want to take the money. "It is not for money that I offer to help you, it is because we are both victims of fascist murderers," he said.

When we got back to the hotel we talked and talked about what to do. I was much more worried than Betty about accepting his offer.

"Listen," she said, "nobody wants us except Brazil. If we go to the consulates in Morocco, why would it be different? I think we should accept his offer."

"So if we are walking on the street, and the police hear us speaking French, and ask for our residence permits, what will we do?" I said. "We don't have a contact to get counterfeit permits. Or if someone like that Nazi who was smiling at the woman with the Swastika necklace found out about us, we could get arrested and put in a prison, or they could send us right back to France."

"We can stay in the apartment most of the time and when we go out, we don't need to talk."

"You are forgetting something — the children. Maybe with Joe, we can explain that we can't go out and he can read and we can play cards with him and it won't be so terrible. But what will we do with Myriam? She will be crying 'I want my bed,' from morning to night. She will drive us crazy sitting home for so long."

"That's true, and when we go out we can be quiet but we can't keep the children, especially Myriam, from talking."

Betty was beginning to change her mind. "From Morocco, I think I would be able to write to my father and get a letter back. He has the address of my cousin William. If only I could get that address — I know he lives on Park Avenue in New York City, but I don't know the number of the building — I would write William a letter and ask him to sponsor us. Then we would have a good chance to go to America."

William was the son of one of Betty's three aunts who had been sent to Ida Grove, Iowa, to find German Jewish husbands. He was the owner of one of the biggest art supply companies in the United States. A very rich man.

◆ ◆ ◆

We decided to go to Morocco and try to get visas from there. So the next morning, we packed and started driving to Algeciras — this is the most southern port in Spain — to take the boat across the straits of Gibraltar. As we drove south, it was getting more and more hot each day, close to one hundred degrees by the time we reached Algeciras, and no air conditioning in our Model T Ford! The children were complaining. "It feels like an oven in here," Joe said. "Are we going to get roasted?" Myriam asked.

"Of course not," Joe said, making a face to say, "I can't believe what a baby she is!" They both kept asking, "How much longer do we have to stay in the car? When will we get on the boat?" We had told them we were going to take a nice boat ride. Betty was busy driving the car, so I was the one who had to keep the children calm. The only good thing was that the heat made them feel so tired that at least some of the time they were sleeping.

We reached Algeciras and stayed overnight. We got a hotel room with lots of windows close by the port, but still it felt like an oven. The hotel had a restaurant downstairs and we were much too tired and hot to go anywhere else, so we sat at a table outside and drank maybe five or six big bottles of mineral water, and ate very little.

The next day, we drove our car on the ferry boat. The trip took a few hours. The straits are only about twenty or thirty miles across, but the waves were very high and a lot of people were getting seasick. Betty and I felt a little bit nauseous. The children were so excited to be on a boat they didn't have time to feel sick. While we were standing on the deck, we started to talk with a very nice Spanish lady who spoke some French. She looked the way we thought all Spanish people looked before we came to Spain. Her hair was black. She had a big pompadour in the front and long hair that was rolled under in the back like the women were wearing in that time. Her eyes were dark chocolate color, and her skin was olive. She had a gift shop in Seville. "I go very often to Morocco to buy pottery, leather bags, wallets, poufs, jewelry, and other stuff for my store," she explained.

She gave us good advice. "The cockroaches in Morocco are about five times as big as anything you have ever seen," she told us. "The most important thing is to find a hotel that doesn't have any or has very few. I will give you some names. When you go shopping, never buy anything without bargaining. This is not Belgium. The shop owners are always asking for at least four, five times what they hope to get. The people selling on the streets are doing the same. Only eat cooked foods, and if you want to have something cold to drink, it has to come out of a sealed bottle, and even the closed bottles it's possible they opened them and put a drink with their water in it. The safest is to drink only hot drinks that have been made with boiled water. You can get very sick in Morocco with amoebic dysentery."

22

THE BOAT LANDED IN Ceuta, in Spanish Morocco. In those times, most of Morocco was French but the North was Spanish. We got into the car and drove off the boat and right away all around us were hundreds of young boys rushing up to the car windows trying to sell us straw hats, sunglasses, bottles of water. Everything was "a bargain, cheap, cheap, very cheap." Others ran up and said, "Guide, guide, need a guide," or "I show you nice hotel." Also very cheap. They knew how to say this in Spanish and French.

Betty and I rolled up the car windows, but it was so hot we couldn't breathe, and the children started complaining, so we had to leave them at least a little bit open. It was very difficult to drive; Betty was afraid she would run over somebody. Joe was very excited, "Look at all the men. They wear long skirts and funny hats on their heads. It's even sunnier here than in Spain; the colors are so bright, and so many palm trees." Myriam was very quiet. Those twenty miles from Spain to Morocco were like two million miles. We were in a different world and she was scared.

A turtle could have crawled through those crowds faster than we drove. But finally we made it out and we were driving down some quiet streets looking for the Hotel *Grande* that the Spanish lady told us about. She even made a little map to show us how to get there.

When we got away from the crowds, Myriam started to feel better. She was looking out the car window, and all of a sudden she cried out, "Look! Look! A lady covered in a bed sheet! Why is the lady covered in a bed sheet?" Surrounding us at the port, and in the cafés around the port, it was only men and boys. Now in the back streets you saw a few women and some of them, you could only see their eyes; everything else was covered. "Maybe they are nuns or beguines," Joe said. "The people here are not Catholic, they are *Musulman*," Betty told him. "They don't have nuns or beguines. The women wear those sheets because their husbands would beat them if they didn't."

I knew that in Arab countries the men were kings. A man could have as many wives as he wanted — well, as many as he could afford — and if he wanted to get rid of one, he only had to say to her, "I divorce you," three times and that was it, finished. Most of the time, the women had to stay at home. That's why the streets and the cafés were filled with men. I had read about this, but I had never seen women covered from head to foot with only the eyes looking out. We saw a lot of very strange things in that year we lived in Morocco. I never dreamt I would see such things in my lifetime.

Even with the map, we got a little bit lost — there were so many tiny narrow streets twisting around — but finally we found the Hotel *Grande* and spent the night there. In the evening, we had dinner in the Spanish restaurant in the hotel. Once again, we were too hot and tired to go anywhere else. I didn't care. Wherever we went, I didn't like the food — paella, tapas, this is not for me. I don't like fancy cooking. I like plain fresh food like we used to eat in Klucze. Boiled potatoes, carrots, flanken, roast chicken, borscht, kugel, kapusniak. Later on, when my children were grown up, always they wanted me to try Chinese, Mexican, all kinds of food I never tasted before, but always I said "no."

Even in Belgium, when we used to go out with friends on Sunday to fancy restaurants, it was hard for me to find something to eat. Sometimes I would order eggs. Sometimes I was sending back the food because it didn't taste fresh. When you grow up on a farm you know what fresh means. Betty was angry about this; she said that I was always making trouble in restaurants.

The next morning, very early, we drove to Tangiers. The city is built on a high cliff that is overlooking the water. "It's so beautiful here," Joe said as soon as we got out of the car, and he ran over to take a better look at the ocean.

"I want to go in the water," Myriam said right away.

"When we get to Casablanca, we will go to the beach and go in the water, not here," Betty told her.

The heat was not yet so terrible, so we took the children for a walk. Right away, they noticed that everywhere were people sitting outside at little card tables, calling out for customers to come over.

"Why are they calling to people?" Joe asked, "They have nothing to sell." Because Tangiers was an international city, free money-trading was legal. Instead of selling tomatoes or sandwiches, these people were selling money! You could buy any currency you wanted. For the children, this was difficult to understand.

After Tangiers, we continued south, and drove through Rabat, toward Casablanca. When we came to Casablanca, we went right away to a hotel that the lady on the boat recommended to us. The manager was an older man, very short — he was standing behind a counter and all you could see was his shoulders and his head. He was wearing very thick glasses. We asked him for a room and gave him our passports.

"So you have come all the way from Poland," he said.

"No," I told him. "We are Polish citizens, but we live in Belgium."

"We have a lot of Jewish refugees from Belgium here," he said.

I think he was trying to find out if we were Jewish. Because our last name was Polish, he wasn't sure. When he found out, he told us, "I am a Jew, too. My family has lived in Morocco since they threw us out of Spain about five hundred years ago."

We were happy to hear that he was Jewish because the first thing we wanted to do after we brought our bags up to the room and washed up a little, was to find out where the refugees were getting together in Casablanca. Right away he told us that there was a Moroccan Jewish club not far away, and the Moroccan Jews had given part of the club to the refugees. When we came back down, he gave us the address and drew us a map — his nose was almost touching the paper when he did this. I think without those thick glasses he was almost blind. So we got in the car and drove to the club. It was about a fifteen-minute walk from the hotel, but it was 100 degrees outside.

We found a place to park right in front of the door. A woman who was walking down the street saw us and came over. She spoke French with a Hungarian accent. "I saw from your license plate that you are coming from Belgium."

"We just arrived today," I told her.

"You are coming to the club?" she asked.

"Yes, as soon as we can wake up our daughter." Myriam had fallen asleep in the back. The heat made her very weak.

"I am from Budapest, but we have a lot of Belgian refugees at the club. They will be happy to see you," she said, and she walked into the building.

We were trying to wake up Myriam when we saw maybe ten people walking out of the club. They took a quick look at our license plate and the letter "B" on the back of the car and they came over to talk to us.

"Welcome to Casablanca."

"Where are you from in Belgium?"

"Are you by any chance from Antwerp?"

"I am from Malines."

"I live in Brussels — Anderlecht."

"When did you get out?"

"How did you get here?"

They were all talking at the same time. We didn't even have a chance to say a word, when we heard someone yell out, "Betty, Henyek!"

Standing in the back of the crowd was Shlomo, the brother of Sammy who was married to Betty's cousin Frieda. We were happy to see someone we knew at least a little bit. By this time, Myriam was awake and crying — she got scared when she saw so many people around the car.

Betty told them, "We will come into the club in a few minutes when the child stops crying."

Only Shlomo stayed. Right away, Betty asked him, "Do you know where Frieda is?"

"Yes, Frieda and Sammy are in Portugal, in Lisbon. I have their address. I can give it to you." Betty was so excited and happy.

As soon as the people left, Myriam stopped crying. We went into the club and we were sitting there for hours. A few people had young children, so Joe and Myriam were playing with them.

Everybody had a story to tell. Some people got out the same way like us — through Spain. Some got out through Marseilles — from there they took a boat. One couple was on a vacation in Nice when Hitler attacked. When they saw that in a few days the Germans were taking over Belgium, they decided not to go back. They went to Marseilles and got out right away — they were the first to get to Morocco.

We asked the people if by any chance they knew a family by the name of Faszczak. We had lost contact with them after Toulouse.

"Certainly, they are old friends of ours from Antwerp," an older couple told us. "They have been here already about two weeks, with their children and their granddaughter. Sometimes they come here and sometimes we see them at the Café de France on the Place de France — this is the other place where the refugees are meeting."

Madame Faszczak and her granddaughter Hélène at the Café de France circa 1944. The Faszcak family spent the entire war years in Morocco.

When we went back to the hotel, we had to park the car a little bit down the street and we saw on one of the buildings an "apartment for rent" sign. We rang the doorbell and a woman in Arab clothes opened the door — her hair was covered, but at least you could see her face. "Yes! I have a nice, furnished one-bedroom apartment on the third floor," she told us. "It is empty. You can see it right now if you want." We went and took a look. It was two medium-size rooms and a small kitchen. The apartment faced another building in the back so it didn't get much sunlight, but this was good. It would be a little cooler than a light apartment. The toilet was in the hallway outside and it was for three apartments on this floor.

One room had a big bed and the other had a sofa. We thought Myriam could sleep on the sofa, and the woman said she had a mattress she could put on the floor for Joe. It was better than being in one hotel room and it was cheaper. We asked her if she would rent it to us by the week and she said "yes."

So the next morning we moved up the street. It was a good thing that we rented this place only for one week. In the middle of the first night, we heard Joe screaming. We ran in. He was standing next to his mattress with his arms hugging each other, and he was trembling.

"What's the matter, what happened?"

"I felt something on my face and I woke up and there was a big, big, black bug on my pillow — it was so dark I don't know if it was a tarantula, or the biggest cockroach in the world. It was horrible, horrible."

We looked all over the floor, but whatever it was we couldn't find it. Joe was too upset to go back to sleep so we sat with him, but he was very tired and finally he couldn't help it and fell asleep. Myriam slept through the whole thing.

The next day, when we opened the French doors between the two rooms all the way, we saw that all the cracks were black with cockroaches. Myriam ran from the door and jumped on the sofa. She covered her eyes with her hands. "It's disgusting, disgusting," she kept saying over and over.

"I don't want to stay in this place," Joe said. "It's horrible. I won't be able to close my eyes tonight."

"Don't worry," Betty said. "We are not going to stay here."

"It could take a few days until we find another place," I told him. "When you go to sleep tonight, I will watch and make sure that no cockroach gets on you, and we will leave a light on all night. The cockroaches like better to come out when it is dark." This made him feel a little better.

The Spanish lady on the boat knew what she was talking about. In my whole life, I have never seen so many cockroaches and such big ones like I saw in Morocco.

◆ ◆ ◆

Later that same day we went to the Café de France. We were sitting there maybe an hour when we saw the Faszczaks come in. We hugged and kissed and then Betty said, "Listen Madame Faszczak, I want to tell you something. My whole life I will be grateful to you because of what you said to me at the bus station in Gaillac. Thanks to you, we all made it into Spain together, and thanks to you, the children and I are here in Casablanca, not in Brussels. I will never forget how you changed our lives with those few words." After the war, when we found out about the concentration camps, we were even more thankful to Madame Faszczak.

We sat with them for hours telling our stories. When we told them about our apartment and the cockroaches, Madame Faszczak said, "We have a nice apartment with very few cockroaches in a good neighborhood, not too far from a park. Why don't you look in the paper for something to rent near us." This is what we did, and a few days later we rented a two-bedroom apartment on rue Admiral Colbert. It had a nice, big living room with a lot of windows — they all had shades you could roll down to keep out the sun — a private toilet, and only once in a while a cockroach.

Many years later Joe went back to Casablanca with his wife, and he was looking and looking, trying to find this street and the building, but he couldn't. When the French left Morocco, the government changed a lot of the street names from French to Arabic.

Now we had an address, so Betty started to write letters. She wrote to her cousin Frieda and right away Frieda wrote back and told her, "Everything here in Portugal is the same as in Morocco. We can't get a visa to the United States, but for the moment we are safe in Lisbon. We can't complain."

She wrote to her father in Belgium and got an answer back. He wrote, "Everything is fine here. We have no shortages of food. I am in good health, busy in my store. Julius is managing your store. Business is not bad. It is already more than three months that the Germans have been here, but they are not bothering anybody. Sam is talking about going to Gaillac to be with Fella, but for the time being he is here working in the store." She had asked her father if he had the address of her cousin William in New York and he sent it to her.

So she wrote to her rich American cousin and asked him to sponsor us to come to America. She never heard back from him. This was a big disappointment. Later on, when we got to New York, William invited us to a dinner. Even now forty years later, Betty and I are still sometimes talking about this dinner.

William lived in such a fancy building there was only one apartment on each floor. When we got out of the elevator we were in his entrance hall and a maid in a uniform was waiting for us. She took us into a living room filled with antiques, and bigger than a lot of people's houses. We shook hands with William and his wife — Germans don't like too much hugging and kissing — and they asked us to sit down. Then they asked the maid to bring us some drinks. I think they were very surprised when I asked for a cup of tea.

We were making conversation. They knew a little bit of French, and some of the time they were speaking German with Betty. They were asking us, "How was your boat trip?" "How old are your children?" "How is your father?" Betty asked them about the other American cousins. Then, after a few minutes, I heard a noise — "quack, quack, quack," — and then I saw coming into the room straight in front of me a white duck. I was thinking to myself, "Am I crazy? Am I dreaming?" In Klucze we had plenty ducks and geese, and chickens running around outside — a *schochet* [person who does ritual slaughtering] would come regularly to slaughter a few — and once in a while one would get into the house and we were chasing it out. But this was Park Avenue in New York City. William could see that Betty and I were staring at this duck. "This is Petie, Helen's pet duck," he told us.

"He's very rich," I was thinking, "but his wife is crazy." When we sat down to dinner, the table was set with flowers and fancy serving dishes, and at least three or four different kinds of glasses, forks, knives, spoons, plates. At such a table, the crazy wife is holding Petie on her lap and feeding him. The duck ate more than I did — every dish had fancy sauces on it, and mushrooms were everywhere.

Finally, when Betty asked William how come he never answered the letter she sent him from Morocco, he told her that he never got the letter. "I was on a business trip to South America at this time," he said. "My secretary must have misplaced the letter." We always suspected he was lying.

For a long time in Morocco, we were running every day to the mailbox looking for a letter from William. We thought he was our only chance to get to America. But in the end we made it without him.

◆ ◆ ◆

When I wrote a letter to my mother and Fella in Gaillac, Fella wrote back right away, "I have not been feeling well; I am having some trouble with my stomach. I have been already three times to the doctor, but he can't figure out what is the matter." When I read this to Betty, she said, "Of course, the doctor can't figure out what is wrong with her — because there is nothing wrong with her," and she was tapping the side of her head with her finger.

My mother wrote, "I have not had any bad heart problems in the last few months; the biggest problem here is the heat. We are not used to this climate. Also I am unhappy with Rifke; she is going out too much at night and coming home late. She says it's not true, but I think she is seeing a young man who is not Jewish."

Later during the war, my mother, Fella, and Rifke were sent by the Vichy government to live in a small town in the Vaucluse called Malaucène. By this time, Sam was with them. From Malaucène, Fella and Sam were sent to Gurs. This was a terrible camp from there they were sending people to Auschwitz. Because Fella and Sam were Canadian citizens, they didn't send them. A few years ago, Fella gave me a poem she wrote about Gurs. She was writing a lot of poems, almost all in Yiddish, but this is the only one she let me see. It was called "A Piece of Bread." I will tell you a few lines in English, "As soon as we came to Gurs, our eyes were swimming in tears.... Our blood froze.... Filth, fear, and death.... Mice and rats.... Surrounded by barbed wire.... If only we could get a piece of bread."

When the war ended, we found out that Rifke had stayed in Malaucène and married a young man from the town. We never saw her again.

23

N OW THAT WE HAD a place to live, we started again to go
to the consulates to try to get visas. It was the same as
in Spain, all we heard was "no, no, no." Even the Brazilians
said "no" — later on they started to change their mind, but by
then we didn't need them anymore.

We wanted very much to get out. Morocco was under the
Vichy French government, and all of us refugees were afraid
that Hitler would come in and take over. After a while we were
hearing stories that the Germans were going to make a camp
in the Sahara Desert to put Jews. This never happened. Hitler
had enough with Auschwitz and Buchenwald and all the other
concentration camps in Germany and Poland.

The weather was a big problem for us — a lot of times, the
wind was blowing in air from the Sahara Desert and it could
go up to 110 degrees Fahrenheit. Myriam was getting very
sick from the heat. She was fainting a lot. If we were walking
with her, we always had to hold her hand very tight in case
she started to fall down. We needed to get out, but nobody
wanted us.

We had enough money to stay in Morocco for a long time.
The cost of living was very, very low. For ten francs, you could
get dinner. Refugees were not allowed to work, so almost every
day in the afternoon, after lunch, I went to the Café de France.
In a room in the back, people were playing chess. I had not
played in a long time — in Brussels, I was working so hard,

186

I didn't have time to play. But here I became a regular in the chess room. One day the chess champion of Morocco came in.

Everybody was very excited and we asked him, "Would you play a few games with the better players?"

"Certainly," he said, "I will be glad to play with them."

When people in the café heard who was playing, a lot of them came over to watch. When it came my turn to play, I beat him. I beat the champion of Morocco! It was a big deal. Everybody was applauding—I was a big shot for a day.

Sometimes I took Joe with me; he was watching me play. One day he said, "*Papy*, I would like to play, too," so I bought a set and I started to play with him. Right away I saw that he had a talent. Later on, Joe played in tournaments. One time, he was tied for first place in the California State Open Championship. He was almost a chess master and even played with Bobby Fischer. By this time, I had stopped playing with him; he was beating me too much.

The Café de France had concerts in the afternoon. A small gypsy-style band played Hungarian *czardas* music and nice French songs by Charles Trenet, Maurice Chevalier, Josephine Baker. Often Madame Faszczak, her daughter Bella, and Betty would rent a horse and buggy and take the children to *Parc* Léauté. (A few weeks after we got to Casablanca, we put an ad in the newspaper and sold our Model T Ford. We were very grateful to this car for taking us all the way from La Panne to Casablanca and we were throwing kisses to it when the new owner drove it away.) Most of the day they stayed in the park in the shade—it was much too hot to stay at home—but then in the late afternoon often Betty would bring Myriam to the café.

We had a woman, Fatma, who was working for us. She was cleaning, shopping, and preparing food. Fatma was with us all that time in Casablanca. She was dressed like they dress over there, but not covering her face. Every day she would come in and take off maybe six, seven *schmattas*. She was a nice woman and one day, after a few months, she asked if she could take Myriam and Joe to meet her family and show them her house. The children wanted very much to go. We liked her very much and we trusted her. She was not a young girl, but a widow maybe forty years old with grown-up children. And we were happy to have a few hours without the children. So we said okay and we asked her to bring them back by six o'clock. At six o'clock we are waiting for them, but nothing; six-thirty, nothing. By a quarter of seven we are getting very worried. Nobody had a telephone in Casablanca and we didn't even know where Fatma lived. By seven-fifteen, we were thinking maybe we should call the police. But then the door opened and the children came running in.

"We had such a good time; it was so much fun," they were telling us. We were so happy to see them, but also angry at Fatma.

"What happened to you? Why are you so late? We were so worried; we almost called the police."

"I'm sorry, I didn't realize you would be worried if we were a little late. The children were enjoying themselves so much. What time is it?"

Fatma didn't have a watch. She always came to work on time, but this was not work and so the time was not so important. After this, we understood that, in Morocco, if you tell a friend you will come at six, it means you will come some time in the evening not very late.

After Fatma left, the children were telling us about her house. They were so excited and they were both talking at the same time. "Can you imagine? There was no furniture in the house, just straw mats. Everybody sits on the floor with their legs crossed," and they sat down on the floor to show us. "In one room there was a little low table in the middle, but no chairs. We had a different kind of very sweet patisserie. It didn't have any chocolate or *crème fraiche*. Fatma said it was made with honey and almonds. It was very good, and we had lemonade — sitting on the floor around the table."

◆ ◆ ◆

We arrived in Morocco in the summer, so we couldn't put Joe in school. He had a lot of time and he liked to collect stamps. He used to stand in front of the post office and go up to people and ask, "May I please have your stamp?" A lot of people would say "yes," and they would rip off the stamps from the envelope they had in their hand. So, after a while, he got a nice collection.

Once he got a stamp from Italy. He came running home; he couldn't wait to show it to us. "Look! Look at the stamp I got! It has a picture of Hitler and Mussolini on it! Two terrible dictators on one stamp."

After a while he had so many stamps he went to a stamp store and sold some of them. He got twelve francs. This was a lot of money for a little boy. I was telling people that here in Morocco my eight-year-old son was making more money than me.

In the fall, we put Joe in school, but he went only for a few days. The French government decided that Casablanca was too crowded with refugees, so they were going to send us to different towns. We were very nervous about where we would have to go. The consulates were in Casablanca. If we couldn't get to a consulate, how could we get a visa? After a few days they announced that they were putting up a list at the Jewish Community Center with all the refugee names and where everybody had to go. Betty went right away to find out where they were sending us. She was standing in the hallway of the center — they put the lists up on the walls — looking for the "M's." When she got to "Miedzianagora," she saw "Safi," and she said out loud, "Safi! That's not so bad."

Next to her was standing a young woman who worked at the Center. She turned to Betty and said, "So you are being sent to Safi."

Betty said "yes" and she started to tell this woman, "I know a very nice man in Belgium, Henri Cohen; he is from Safi. He always used to tell us what a nice place it is, and that he has a lot of family living there...."

Before Betty could say another word, the young woman interrupted her: "My name is Françoise Cohen. Henri Cohen is my uncle."

When Betty came home that day, she was very excited. She told me what happened: "You know me. I always have something to say, but when this young woman told me she was Henri's niece, I was just standing there with my mouth open! If I saw such a coincidence in a movie, I wouldn't believe it. Françoise was very friendly. Right away she invited me to her office. We sat down; she made some mint tea. I told her that Henri works in our shoe store in Brussels, and that last year he married your cousin Golda — she looked very surprised when I said this. She told me that she lives with her parents in Casablanca, but she goes sometimes to Safi to visit the family. It is about 250 kilometers south of Casablanca. Also she told me that two of her uncles who are deaf-mutes have a nice big house there and maybe we could rent a room from them. She gave me their address."

24

SAFI IS A SMALL town on the ocean with a lot of fishermen and sardines, also they make nice pottery. When we got there, we went right away to the deaf-mute brothers' house. Françoise gave Betty the address, but she didn't tell her that their house was in the casbah. When we walked through the gate to the casbah and started looking for it, we almost turned around. Already it was very hard to get used to living in Morocco, but at least in Casablanca we had an apartment in a nice modern neighborhood with wide streets. Now we were walking through streets that were maybe ten feet wide, and they felt even narrower because all the stores — it didn't matter if they were selling fruit and vegetables or fixing shoes — had stands on the streets. Besides the stands, everywhere people were squatting against the houses and selling all kinds of foods, clothes, and leather goods out of big straw baskets. Everybody was yelling what bargains they had — when they saw us they yelled in French. The streets were so crowded with people and donkeys carrying merchandise in big bags on their backs, sometimes we had to stop and wait for a few minutes to have room to take a few steps. If you took a look up at the sky, you were closed in, too — a lot of the houses had little terraces overlooking the streets. Many of the stores had awnings and they were hanging bananas and grapes and all kinds of stuff on them. Joe was very excited by all this, but Myriam was scared. "I don't like it here," she was saying. "Too many people. I want to leave."

"Maybe we should get out of here right now. We are not going to live in this place," I said to Betty.

"Listen, Françoise wrote to the brothers, and they are expecting us. We are already here, why don't we at least go and meet them? You can put Myriam on your shoulders."

This is what I did, and right away she stopped complaining. I took a look at my watch. "Let's try to find the house," I said, "but if we are still wandering around the casbah in ten minutes, we will leave." We agreed on this and continued. We asked maybe half a dozen people for directions before we found the house. We rang the doorbell and a man dressed in the Moroccan style with the white skirt and a fez on his head came and let us in. Even before we said anything, he knew who we were.

"The Cohen brothers will be happy to see you," he told us. "My name is Mohammed and I speak for them."

The entrance hall was small, and right in front of us was the staircase. It was decorated with tiles with nice designs in a lot of different colors — like the Spanish-style houses in Los Angeles. This man led us up the stairs to a long hall. The hallway floor was also made of tiles, but they were big and beige with black decorations around each one. The walls were painted a nice yellow color. Everything inside looked very clean and happy.

We came into the living room and the two brothers were sitting on a low sofa without armrests. They were also dressed in the Moroccan style. They stood up and shook hands with us.

The room had handmade carpets on the floor. They were not thick, wool carpets like we had in Brussels, but were made of cotton, and like the hallway floor, they were filled with designs in beautiful colors. The furniture was not what we were used to, but at least they had chairs. We were glad we didn't have to sit on pillows on the floor. The brothers were very friendly, smiling a lot. They were talking in sign language to Mohammed, and he told us what they were saying. One of them even got up and showed the children a bellows and he let them play with it. They were having a lot of fun blowing air at each other.

Mohammed brought in some tea and those very sweet little Moroccan cakes. After a while they said, "Now we will show you the room." We followed them and Mohammed up some more stairs. The room was a nice size, maybe fifteen by twenty feet.

"We have beds for all of you," they told us. "The W.C. is in the hall, but you would be the only ones using it. We have another W.C. on our floor. We have a little charcoal stove we don't use anymore, so we could put it in the room for you."

Also they showed us a courtyard on the same floor where we could sit or the children could play when it was not too hot. They asked for very little money. I whispered to Betty (I didn't want Mohammed to hear me), "This place looks very, very clean."

"I haven't seen one cockroach," she said. "And we have nowhere else to stay right now."

"Let's ask them if we could stay for one week and we will look for an apartment with a separate bedroom."

"I agree. Let's see what they say."

"You can stay for one night or for one year. Whatever you wish," they told us.

After the first week we got used to living in the casbah. And in the end we lived in this room for five months. There were only a few one-bedroom apartments for rent in the town and by the time we started to look, most of them were already taken by the other refugees. We didn't regret staying with the Cohen brothers. The inside of their house was much nicer and cleaner than where the other refugees were living; they were always complaining about the cockroaches and we had very few. Myriam and Joe were sleeping on one side of the room and we were on the other side.

Myriam in Safi in 1999, in front of the house where the family lived

The fruit stand in front of the house, 1999

If we needed something from the brothers, or if we had a problem or a question, and Mohammed was not there to talk sign language, we wrote everything down and they wrote back in a perfect French.

We were the only refugees in Safi who had Moroccan family! We were invited a few times by Henri's nephews and nieces to have dinner with them on Friday night. We were very surprised when they told us that Henri had a wife in Morocco and five children. He had not told us anything about this. We never found out exactly what was the truth. Was he divorced? Separated? Did he abandon his family? It was hard to believe this about him. Only one thing we knew for sure — he was a very good husband to Golda.

There was a small square with a park just outside the casbah, and we used to spend a lot of time there with the other refugee families. All the time we were talking about the political-military situation. What would the Germans do next? Would they attack North Africa? Could they defeat the Russians? Would the Americans fight against the Germans? Even Joe was interested in politics. He was only eight-and-a-half years old, but he was very smart and the older men were talking with him. One day, they asked his opinion and he said, "I think that the Germans are going to try to go through Egypt and the Middle East and go to India!" Where he got such an idea I don't know!

By November/December the weather started to get cooler. One Friday afternoon, we took the children for a walk in the neighborhood where the rich people lived. We saw that outside the gates to a few of the houses servants were sitting on low stools, and people — you could see from the way they were dressed that they were very poor — were waiting in line. When they got to the front of the line, they put out their hand and the servant put some money in. We walked around for a while and when we saw that there was no one in line in front of one of the houses, we went over and asked the man at the gate, "We noticed that you are giving money to poor people. Is it some special occasion?"

"The special occasion is *Shabbat*," he said. "I work for Jews, and every Friday afternoon they send me out to sit here at the gate and give money to poor Jews so that at least once a week they have a good meal." Most Moroccan Jews were very poor.

The rich Moroccan Jews were giving charity to us refugees, too — they fixed up a little community center for us. I use to go there to play chess, and sometimes Joe would come with me. Most of the time he was watching and sometimes I would play with him. He wasn't coming with me as much as in Casablanca because he was going to school.

In Safi, there was a Muslim school, a French school, and a Jewish school. We decided to send Joe to the *école Israelite*. It was on top of a hill overlooking the casbah and the town. The hill was red clay, so soft that you could stick your hand in the ground and scoop it up. It was very good for making pottery, but not for growing food. Joe walked to school.

The first day he went to school, we were waiting and waiting for him to come home. After a while, we got worried and I said to Betty, "I will go to the school; maybe they are keeping the children later today," and I started walking toward the hill. To get in and out of the casbah you always had to walk through a big stone arch. When I got to the arch that was close to the hill, I saw a lot of people watching a snake charmer. He was sitting on the ground on a small rug and playing music on something that looked like a flute. The snake was lifting itself out of a box. I didn't see Joe right away. He and a few other boys were standing near the front with a lot of people behind them. I got through the crowd and tapped him on the back. He jumped and turned around when he saw me, his eyes and mouth wide open.

"We were getting worried about you," I said, "so I came to look for you."

"I didn't realize how long I was here!" He didn't need to say anymore. I could see he was so enchanted with the show, he forgot everything. I watched a few minutes with him, and then I took him home. I knew that Betty would be happy to see him. After that we never worried if he was late; we knew where we could find him. Besides snake charmers, there were musicians and sometimes fire-eaters at the gate.

Joe's school was mostly Moroccan Jewish boys, and a few refugee children. The teachers used to slap the Moroccan boys if they didn't behave the way they were supposed to. One day one of the Belgian refugee boys did something the teacher didn't like and the teacher slapped him. The next day the father of this boy came to school and slapped the teacher very hard across the face. After that, they never hit any of the refugee children again.

One time, Joe came home from school and he was very upset. He told us that a Moroccan boy about fourteen or fifteen years old was playing hooky for about three weeks, but he came back to school that day. The principal came into the room and told the boy to stand up. Then he told four of the biggest boys in the class to grab him. They took his shoes off and the principal took a square, steel rod and was hitting this boy on the soles of his feet. "It was horrible, horrible," Joe was saying over and over.

Many years later, we were already living in Los Angeles, Joe and I were remembering about Morocco and he told me about things that happened to him in Safi. "One day one of the Moroccan boys at the school came up to me and said '*schmeckel in tuchus* [penis in butt]?' I didn't understand what he was talking about. It was the first time I heard anything about sex — you and mom never talked about it." (This is true; we never said anything to Joe or Myriam about sex. It was not like now when all they are talking about on the television is sex; people never talked about such things in those days.)

"I knew the Yiddish meaning," Joe told me, "but it didn't make sense to me. The boy repeated it — he must have learned how to say this in Yiddish from one of the refugee boys — and smirked and I just let it go. I thought he was out of his mind. Luckily no one ever tried to push that on me."

Mostly, Joe remembered good things: "One day there was a torrential downpour; it must have been in the late fall. I started walking home from school and I got totally soaked. And then about half-way home, I saw you coming. You were carrying a big umbrella and wearing a big overcoat. You took me under your overcoat and we walked back home. I always remembered that — it gave me a very warm good feeling, like you were protecting me."

He also remembered having shoes made to order: "I guess there were very few shoe stores or maybe none at all. You took me to this place where they took measurements and they made me this very nice pair of shoes. I still remember the smell of the leather. On the same street as the shoemaker, there was a little movie theater — the only one in town — and the woman who sold the tickets was a relative of the deaf-mute brothers in whose house we lived. She knew us and liked us, so when Myriam and I went there sometimes on Saturday or Sunday we would make-believe we were giving her money and she would give us tickets for free."

Once I asked Myriam what she remembered about Morocco, and she said, "The circular slide in the playground in Casablanca; at the beach, running on sand that was burning my feet; a pretty waitress with black hair who served me chocolate pudding." She doesn't remember how sick she was.

Morocco was such a poor country and so dirty. Wherever you went there were flies. People — some of them blind — were sitting on the ground begging or selling vegetables or other things and flies were all over their faces. Maybe this is why Myriam got so sick. She was fainting all the time from the heat and she got amoebic dysentery, blood in her stools. Betty took her to see a French doctor. She told Betty, "You better take this child out of the country because I don't know if she's going to survive here. She is not meant for this climate." It's a good thing we got out of Morocco pretty soon after that. Myriam helped us to get out — she was not only sick; she was also good at making-believe she was sick.

25

AFTER WE WERE IN Safi maybe five months, we got a letter from Frieda. She wrote, "Here in Lisbon the American consulate has started to give visas to some refugees. The immigration regulations have been changed. Now some people who are at the bottom of the quota list are allowed to take the place of others who have been registered for many years but cannot get out of their country. For the first time we are feeling optimistic; maybe we will be seeing each other soon in America." When we heard this, we got very excited. There was still a chance we might get visas to Brazil, but we preferred very much to go to the United States. We wanted to go right away to the American consulate. So we went to the local *préfecture* and got a permit to go for a few days to Casablanca.

When we got to the American consulate, they told us, "Yes, the rules have been changed, and it is possible you might be able to get visas." So we went back to Safi and applied for a *carte de séjour* — a permit to spend time in Casablanca. We wanted to be close to the consulate in case we had to fill out some papers, or maybe they needed more information from us. Also we wanted to make sure they didn't forget about us. They gave us a permit for a limited time. So we packed our few things and went to Casablanca. We rented a room in a hotel in the casbah — it cost less and we had already gotten used to this kind of living. The streets were a little wider than in the Safi casbah.

The owner of the hotel was French, Monsieur Fontaine. He was very nice, and against the fascists, but once in a while he would say something antisemitic. We had Polish passports and our name was Miedzianagora, so he had no idea that we were Jewish. I didn't say a word; the hotel was very clean, very few cockroaches; Joe was having a nice time playing with his daughter — they were about the same age. I figured so many *goyim* are at least a little bit antisemitic, so Monsieur Fontaine is saying what they are thinking.

I was talking with Monsieur Fontaine every day about the political situation. When Germany attacked Russia on June 22, 1941, we made a toast to a Russian victory. He said, "If the Russians survive until the winter, the Germans are lost." I agreed with him, and we were right.

◆ ◆ ◆

At the hotel we couldn't cook very much. For lunch — this was the big meal — we went to a restaurant where it cost nine francs per person, even less for Myriam. The waitress was a very good-looking, tall young woman with very dark, brown hair made up in a pompadour on top of her head — it was the style in those days. Her name was Leila and she was very friendly. We left her a nice tip and she served us extra portions. For breakfast or supper, Betty fixed something in the room on a little charcoal stove. One day she asked Joe to go and buy some charcoal for cooking. He came back upset and told us, "There was a really long line, fifty to one hundred people, and a French gendarme was controlling it. He was really nasty. He was yelling at the Arab people to stay in a straight line. If they got out of line, he stepped on their toes and a lot of people didn't wear shoes. When he saw me he didn't say a word. He just grabbed my arm and took me to the front of the line and I got the charcoal right away."

We were waiting for the American visas, but our permit to stay in Casablanca was expiring. They gave us one extension without trouble, but when Betty went back for a second extension the French official said, "No, you have to go back to Safi." She was begging him to give us a little more time, but again he said "no." So Betty made up a story. She said, "Listen, my little girl Myriam is very, very sick; she has a terrible sore throat and a very high fever and she can't be moved."

He told her, "I don't believe you and I am going to get in my car right now and go to your hotel. If you are lying, you will have to wait a very, very long time before you ever get another permit to come to Casablanca."

Betty answered him very calmly, "Okay, I'll see you back at our residence." Later, she told me that in her whole life she never felt her heart beat so fast.

She ran out of the building and was lucky she got a taxi right away, so she arrived at the hotel before the French official. She ran into our room and grabbed a bottle with some blue medicine inside — people used to smear this on the tonsils and the throat for sore throats. She grabbed Myriam and tried to paint her throat with it, but Myriam started screaming and crying, so a lot of this blue stuff got on her lips and around her mouth. Betty put her in bed and told her to stay there. While she was doing all this, she was explaining to me what had happened.

A couple of minutes later, the official comes in and takes a look. Myriam is lying in bed screaming, with this blue stuff on her face, so he says, "Pardon me, *Madame,* I made a mistake; I can see now that your daughter is very sick. I will give you an extension for two weeks." We waited a few minutes and then we took Myriam out of bed and washed her face. We told her that she could have an extra, fancy dessert when we went for lunch. At the restaurant, we asked the waitress to put some whipped cream and a cookie on top of her chocolate pudding.

While we waited to see the American consul, we had a routine: we went to our restaurant for lunch, then back to the hotel for the hottest part of the day — we had a fan and at least we were in the shade — and then around three or four o'clock we would go to the park. Sometimes we went to the

The Miedzianagora family in Casablanca, Spring, 1941

beach. Betty and the children went in the water; I don't like to get wet. Later in the afternoon, we were going almost every day to the Café de France. I was playing chess in the back and most of the time Joe was watching. Sometimes I played with him. I was still beating him in those days. Betty was sitting in the café with Myriam and the Faszczak and some of the other refugees.

One day, at last they let us in to see the United States consul. We had given a nice present to the receptionist, so she moved our date up a few months. We told the consul that we have $10,000 in the bank in New York City, and we paid five hundred francs so he would cable First National City Bank. When the answer came back, he said, "Okay, I can give you a visa." It was one of the happiest days of our lives. But we still had a very big problem — how to get to America.

One day, I was sitting on a bench in the *Parc* Léauté watching the children. A Moroccan man, about the same age as me, sat down next to me, and I started a conversation with him. I enjoy meeting people like this. I still do it when I have a chance. He told me that he had his own travel agency. I saw him a few times after that, and always we had a nice talk. So now we went to see him in his office.

First, he tried to get us on a French boat going from Casablanca to Martinique and then to New York, but the boat was already full. So then we promised him two hundred dollars and we would pay all his expenses if he would go to Madrid to try to get us on a Spanish boat. It didn't take him long to say "yes" — it was a lot of money in those days. "I cannot go immediately," he told us. "I have to arrange for my brother to be in the office while I am gone and I have to take care of a few things before he takes over." We could see he was worried — he was leaning his elbow on his desk and rubbing his forehead over and over — and we knew why. He had told me in one of our conversations that his brother Ali helped him in his agency, but Ali was an alcoholic, so he couldn't trust him too much. But for $200 it was worth taking a chance.

A few days later, Hassan left for Madrid. A few days after he left, I started to go by the office every day to see if there was any news. One morning, I walk in and Ali tells me, "You are a very lucky man. Hassan came back from Spain last night and he has tickets for you on a boat to New York, the *Marques de Comillas* leaving July 5 from Vigo, Spain. Your wife and children have to stay on the top of the boat in a little hospital they have in case of contagious diseases."

I said, "Fine, this is not a problem." We would have slept outside on the deck if we had to.

The tickets were very cheap. I still remember the prices: $150 each for me and Betty, $84 for Joe, and $42 for Myriam. I told Ali I would get the money and come back in a little while. Just as I am getting up to go, he takes out a bottle of Calvados from behind his desk and he says,

"How about a little drink to celebrate?"

I said, "Thank you very much, I would like to make a toast with you, but my doctor told me I could get very sick if I drink alcohol." I said this because I didn't want to offend him.

Betty and I celebrated together — we went to the Café de France that afternoon and told our refugee friends that we had boat tickets for New York, and we bought coffee, *patisseries,* ice cream — whatever they wanted — for everybody. Around this time, the German army was already in Libya and Egypt — only about seven or eight hundred miles away — so all of us refugees were very scared that they were going to take over Morocco. But now we had visas and boat tickets and if the Germans invaded, by then we would be in New York.

We still had one problem. When we first arrived in Morocco, we had to declare how much money we had. The French government took away our dollars and gave us an "I owe you," and some French francs — *schmattas* worth nothing outside of France and its territories. Now that we were leaving, we made a trip to Rabat to talk to government officials about getting our dollars back. First we thought we would leave the children with some refugee friends, but then we thought if we have two small children with us, maybe they will be more sympathetic.

◆ ◆ ◆

We got in to speak to the Finance Minister. He had a very big office, so we put the children down in one corner on those Moroccan poufs — they liked very much to sit on them — and we gave Joe some books to read to Myriam. First the minister said he couldn't release any of our dollars, but we kept arguing with him, and at least he didn't throw us out of his office. Then all of a sudden we hear Joe yell out, "*Mamy, papy,* I think Myriam is going to faint again." We ran over and I picked her up and walked back to the minister's desk. Now I was sitting with Myriam on my lap. She didn't faint but she felt very drowsy and she was soaking wet from the heat. "Is there anything I can do for the child?" the minister asked. "If you have a glass of cold water, I have a clean handkerchief, and I will wipe her face and body a little bit," Betty said. "She faints all the time from the heat." His secretary brought us the water, and soon after this he agreed to let us take back most of the dollars we had brought into the country with us.

26

I T WAS THE END of June when we took the train in Casablanca to go to Spain. The first stop was Rabat. The children were very thirsty and Betty wanted to buy them some lemonade, so she got off the train and went to the kiosk. A few seconds later, the train began to move out of the station. Myriam and Joe started screaming so loud you could hear them in every wagon. I pulled the alarm to stop the train.

A conductor came in. I told him, "My wife got off in Rabat to buy lemonade...."

"*Calmez vous, calmez vous,*" he said. "We are changing the locomotive — we take the train out a kilometer and then we bring it back."

When we heard this we started to breathe again. We felt even better when Betty got back on the train. The children were jumping all over her and screaming, "*Mamy, mamy.*" Betty told us, "I wasn't worried at all because as soon as the train started to pull out, the man in the kiosk told me they do this all the time and the train is coming back in a few minutes." After that, for months to come, even when we were in America, the children didn't want Betty to leave the house.

So with Betty on the train again, we continued north to Algeciras. From there, we got on the boat and crossed the Straits of Gibraltar to Cadiz. From Cadiz we took a train to Madrid. During the Spanish Civil War, some trains had been bombed and many had not yet been fixed. Soon after we got on the train it started to rain. We were lucky, there was no hole over our seats. Some people were sitting and holding umbrellas, but when I went to the toilet with Joe it was pouring and the floor was flooded.

It was nighttime when we got to Madrid. We went back to the same hotel where we had stayed the last time. Consuela, the owner's daughter, was at the desk when we came in. She was so happy to see the children. She ran over to hug them. It was almost a year since we had stayed there. Joe remembered her very well. Myriam was too young. She got a little scared. "Who is that lady? Why did she hug me?" she asked.

The next morning, I got up very early and went to the train station. The boat was leaving in a few days, and I had to get tickets to Vigo. I got to the ticket counter about a half-hour before it opened. I was the first in line. Soon there were about thirty or forty people behind me, and they were all speaking in Spanish. The man standing right behind me started talking to me and this is how he found out that I was not Spanish. I saw him turn around and say something to the person behind him. Pretty soon people were whispering and shaking their heads. I could feel it was bad. Then a policeman came over. He didn't say a word, he just took me by the arm and put me at the end of the line. So I waited maybe two hours, but still I was lucky. When I got to the ticket counter, they had a few first-class tickets left to Vigo. Right after I got them, they closed the window.

◆ ◆ ◆

On July 5, 1941 — almost one year and two months after we left Brussels — we climbed up the gangplank to the *Marques de Comillas*. We had two new little suitcases that we bought in the casbah just before we left Casablanca. We didn't want to arrive in New York looking like *schnorrers* [beggars] with dirty, ripped-up luggage. Betty was holding the children's hands and I was carrying the suitcases. I went first with them to their cabin all the way on the top of the ship. It was supposed to be an isolation ward in case somebody got a contagious disease. I don't know what they would have done if someone really got a contagious disease. Maybe they would have put up a curtain and put Betty and the other women and children in part of the lounge. But it didn't happen. They spent the whole trip in a big sunny cabin — it had a lot of portholes — with regular beds for eight people.

When I got to my cabin it was a different story. They put me in the bottom of the boat in a dormitory with about twenty other men. It was so dark, it felt like the middle of the night. The bunks were so close, one on top of the other, I could see right away that when I got up in the morning I had to be very careful not to hit my head. Betty and the children came down with me to see the cabin. The children wanted to know exactly where I was going to be. Myriam was upset that I wouldn't be in the same cabin with them. She was saying over and over, "Why can't *papy* stay upstairs with us? I want him to stay with us." We explained to her that upstairs was only for ladies and girls, but then she said, "But Jojo is a boy and he is staying upstairs. So why can't *papy* stay upstairs too?"

Finally, Betty told her to stop it, "Listen, *papy* can't stay with us. That's how it is. I don't want to hear you ask one more time!"

In normal times, I would have been very upset to have to sleep for more than two weeks in a place like this, but I was so happy to be out of Morocco, away from Hitler, and going to New York that it was not such a big deal.

It was a beautiful ship. When we walked into the dining room, we saw the tables were covered with white tablecloths and cloth napkins. Crystal chandeliers were hanging from the ceiling. It was the same feeling like when we got to the Ritz Hotel in Barcelona. The food was very good — even I liked it — and at four o'clock they served cookies and lemonade for the children. Many years later, Myriam told me that the only thing she remembered from the boat was the beautiful dining room and a long table with a white tablecloth and cookies and lemonade.

It took only a few days and Myriam became healthy. She wasn't fainting anymore; she was running around playing with the other children. Joe, too, made friends with kids his age, but sometimes we were sitting in the lounge playing chess. One day, a very well-dressed Spanish man was kibitzing and was very impressed that a nine-year-old boy could play like this. The next day he asked Joe to play a game. After that, they were playing often. One day, we found out that this man was the Spanish consul in Havana.

There was a man on the boat who was always with a nurse and whenever he sat down he would take pieces of paper and rip them up into tiny, tiny, little pieces. Joe's chess partner told him that this man had very bad shell shock from the Spanish Civil War. He was from a wealthy family and they were sending him to stay with family in Cuba. They hired a nurse to watch over him. Maybe they were afraid he would try to jump into the ocean.

One time at night, in the middle of the Atlantic there was a terrible storm — the boat was rocking back and forth like it was going to turn over and everybody was seasick and vomiting. In the morning, Betty told me that one of the women in her cabin had been making her and everyone else crazy. The woman was so scared, the whole night she was moaning and crying and praying very loud in Hebrew. They couldn't get her to stop.

I had a bigger problem. One night, I was sleeping on my bunk and I felt a little tickling. I woke up and I saw the tail of a rat. I jumped off the bed, grabbed my stuff, and went up to the lounge and that is where I slept every night after that.

That first night, when I went up to the lounge, I walked out on the deck to get a little fresh air first. It was the middle of the night and everybody was asleep, so I was surprised that the lights all over the ship were still on. There was a war going on and there were German submarines in the Atlantic. Some of the lights were even in different colors. It looked like Christmas time in the United States. The next morning, I asked a ship man about this and he told me that the captain kept the lights on the whole night because he did not want the German submarines to think that the ship was English and sink us. He wanted them to see right away that it was a neutral Spanish ship.

After about ten days on the Atlantic, we stopped in Havana, Cuba, for a few days, but the Cubans wouldn't let us out. By then, we had given up our Polish citizenship because it had become better to be stateless, and the Cuban government was afraid they would be stuck with us. This was very stupid. Why would we want to stay in Cuba when we had visas to go to America?

Finally, we left Havana. One morning, after a few days, we were sitting in the dining room finishing breakfast, when we heard a lot of yelling outside. We knew that we would be arriving in New York on this day, but we thought it would be later in the afternoon. Betty jumped up from the table. "It's possible we are arriving early. I will go and find out." In a few minutes, she came back very excited. "We are already entering the port of New York," she told us. We took the children and we ran up on the highest deck. It was very crowded, but we found a place on the railing, on the left side of the boat. Everybody was looking for the tall buildings, but we couldn't see any. When you come into New York, first you see Staten Island on the left and Brooklyn on the right, but we didn't know this. We all thought that right away you see Manhattan and the skyscrapers.

Next to us was standing an older Jewish couple from Frankfurt. Sometimes, Betty and I were sitting in the lounge talking with them. The lady was very nervous; always she was blinking her eyes and rubbing her hands. One time, I met her husband on the deck. We were talking, and he told me, "My wife has not always been like this. She was a happy woman before the Nazis took away our Germany." Now she was sounding very worried. "Our children are waiting for us in New York City," she said to her husband. "Perhaps the captain has decided to land in another city. What shall we do? How will they find us?"

"*Schatzi* [darling], wherever we land we are safe now, and the children will find us," he told her. "You don't need anymore to worry so much."

A few minutes later, we could see the Statue of Liberty, and she was yelling, "*Die Freiheitsstatue! Die Freiheitsstatue!*"

"So now you believe that we are in New York?" her husband asked her. She looked at him and started to cry.

Everybody was yelling in their language "*freiheitsstatue,*" "*la statue de la liberté,*" "*statuia libertati.*" Some people were already practicing English and saying "statue of liberty."

"Why is everybody yelling so much about a statue?" Myriam asked.

"Because it is a statue of a lady who welcomes everybody to America," Betty told her. When we got very close to the statue, I put Myriam on my shoulders. She started to wave and she said, "*Bonjour, madame.*"

Joe looked up at her and said, "It's a statue, silly, it's not a real person."

"I know that it's a statue," Myriam said, "but I want to say '*bonjour*' to her anyway."

On the right side of the boat, you could now see the skyscrapers of Manhattan, and soon the boat was docking. A lot of people were crying and everybody who had family or friends in America was looking to see if they could recognize someone in the crowd standing behind a green fence, waving. We looked and looked and then we saw family from Belgium who got to America before us — Frieda and Sammy, and Betty's cousin Bertha, her husband, Leon, and their son Gaston, who was just a few years older than Joe. My sister Nachele who lived in Brooklyn since the 1920s was not there, but when we got off the boat, we met her son-in-law Max. She had sent him to get us.

Max didn't have a car, so he took us in a taxi. The cousins from Belgium came with us to the taxi, but then they said, "We will meet you by the family in Brooklyn in about a half-hour. We are already New Yorkers, we are taking the subway," and they waved good-bye.

We started driving to Bensonhurst in Brooklyn. Myriam looked out the window and said, "The buildings are so tall they touch the sky."

"How do they keep them from falling down?" Joe asked.

Betty and I looked at each other and at the same time we both said, "*Mazel tov*. We are in New York City. We are in America."

The Miedzianagora family in Central Park, Summer, 1941

Family Portrait, New York City, circa 1945

Family Portrait, New York City, circa 1945

Epilogue

A FEW YEARS AGO, I heard a radio interview with Richard Breitman, a professor of German history at American University, in which he talked about the revelation that Anne Frank's father had made numerous and futile efforts to get visas to the U.S. for his family. The Frank family was viewed as a threat to U.S. national security because they had relatives living in Germany! "Anne Frank could have been a seventy-seven-year-old woman living in Boston today — a writer," I heard Professor Breitman say. "And I, a writer living in New York, could have been hidden in an attic in Brussels, and killed at Bergen Belsen," I thought to myself, were it not for my father's extraordinary foresight, and both my parents' courage, survival skills, and occasional luck. Instead, I spent from 1941 to 1946 living on Manhattan's Upper West Side, in the heart of the Belgian refugee enclave that ran from about 96th Street to 105th Street on and around Central Park West.

After only a few days in New York, my father was ready to buy a house in Bensonhurst, across the street from where we were staying with his family. My mother was always grateful to her cousin Frieda for a narrow escape from what she viewed as a deadly boring life in Brooklyn. (The Brooklyn of 1941 was a far cry from the gentrified trendy borough that young people flock to today.)

"I was very lucky," she would tell us in later years when she was reminiscing. "Frieda took me aside, and told me that we have to come to Manhattan and see where they are living before we make any decision about buying a house in Brooklyn." My parents opted for sharing a second floor apartment with Frieda and her husband in an old tenement that still stands at the corner of 100th Street and Central Park. For most of the year, the park served as a social center for refugees, and a playground for their children. In the winter, my mother took us sled-riding and skating on the small lake nearby.

Antwerp was and still is a very Jewish world-diamond center, so my father didn't have much trouble getting a job in the Yiddish-speaking diamond industry — there wasn't much else he could do, since he didn't speak English. He hated the work, and in later years always complained about how cutting diamonds had had a very bad effect on his nerves. My mother became a housewife for five years. To her — she had started to work full-time at the age of fourteen — it seemed like a wonderful vacation. She studied English, and joined a refugee group that provided support work — a lot of knitting blankets and sweaters — for soldiers.

My brother went to the local elementary school on 103rd Street and Amsterdam, and I eventually joined him there. I had nothing to compare it to, but he found school in New York to be wonderfully lenient and easygoing compared to his very strict and rigid Belgian elementary school. And so, when we moved back to Belgium in June 1946, he wanted to stay in New York and my parents agreed. He spent the first year living with a close friend and his family, and then boarded at Horace Mann in Riverdale, at the time a school for boys. He spent the summers with us in Brussels, and at Knokke-Le-Zoute, a resort town on the seashore, near Holland.

My parents and I moved back into our Brussels apartment. The Germans had removed all our furniture, and the rooms were barren, furnished mostly with a few items my parents had shipped from our tiny New York apartment. The central heating was not yet working that first freezing winter of 1946–1947. and we used a few coal stoves to provide a bit of warmth. I remember getting dressed in the morning in bed, under the blankets.

Betty, Henyek, and Myriam – with her dog Skippy – in front of
their Uccle apartment building at 242, Avenue Coghen

Henyek with his mother on the apartment terrace, circa 1947

Betty and Henyek in front of their shoe store at 4, rue St. Catherine

Besides my grandmother, who was very sick and mostly bedridden, my father's half-brother Shaya and his wife lived with us for a while — they had survived the war, but lost their apartment. Shaya, a very gentle and patient man, taught me French over the summer. My mother, probably wanting to practice her English, had stopped speaking French to us; my father spoke mostly Yiddish. By the time I entered fifth grade in the *école Communale d'Uccle,* in the fall, I was fluent. My French just needed a little coaxing to come back.

My parents got back their store, which had been taken over by a Belgian fascist, and business was booming. They imported shoes from the U.S. — European manufacturers were just getting started again.

They must have been devastated to find out that the entire Polish family had been wiped out, and that my mother had lost her brother. But they never talked about it or showed any emotion in front of me. Or if they did, I blocked it out.

In 1951, my parents moved to Los Angeles. They had visited a few years earlier after my mother received a letter from Tsilli, a Belgian refugee friend who had moved there with her family. Tsilli described the perfect weather and informed my mother that, unlike New York, in Los Angeles you never needed to wear a hat. The combination did it for my mother. I think my father was more ambivalent; in many ways he preferred life in Belgium.

Prior to the move, my parents sold their Brussels property, but kept their store run by my grandfather, my step-grandmother, and Madame Rita, the manager.

By 1951, I had fully readjusted to living in Belgium and was having a great time at my high school, *l'Athénée d'Uccle.* The last thing I wanted was to move again, and Los Angeles represented the ultimate in culture shock. Fortunately as far as I was concerned, for the next ten years my parents spent half the year in Brussels and half the year in L.A. They feared going into business in the U.S.; both the business culture and the potential customers were so different from what they were used to in Europe. Their store in Brussels was still thriving, so they returned every year. I got to go back every summer, and eventually spent two years at the Sorbonne in Paris.

In 1961, my parents finally gave up their store and from then on lived in Los Angeles where they bought some properties and semi-retired. From 1963 until they passed away — my father at age 94, my mother at age 92 — they lived on North Gardner Street in an apartment facing the Hollywood hills, with the Hollywood sign on the right, the apartment where at the beginning of this book my father is sitting and writing his "memoir."

In the early 1980s, Henyek on the floor, having fun with Myriam,
and granddaughters Debbie, Alisa, and Nadia

Henyek celebrating his ninetieth birthday,
Nadia and Alisa at his side

Henyek with Debbie shortly before he passed away

Afterword

I MUST ADMIT THAT for many years, I viewed the survival stories that make up this book as nothing special. Children tend to take for granted the environment and family histories that they grow up with. Years ago, I met a woman who had eighteen-month-old twins; she told me that she had recently taken her children to visit a friend and her newborn baby. Her twins ran around the apartment looking in every corner for "the other one." I have always remembered this story because it captures so succinctly and clearly how we view as normal whatever we grow up with. I grew up hearing stories of escaping death by execution, and running from Nazis. No big deal!

I did not give much thought either when I was young to how difficult it must have been for my parents, who had grown up in Northern Europe and were living in a twelve-room apartment in Brussels when the war started, to spend six months in one room with two young children in a casbah alley in a small Moroccan town where the temperature could go up to 110 degrees Fahrenheit.

In my case, the tendency to take for granted one's childhood background, to not ask questions or reflect on it, was undoubtedly intensified by the fact that until the early 1980s I did not in any conscious way allow the Holocaust into my life. I avoided all books, films, and TV shows about it. In 1982, I took my first step towards facing the horror — I went to see Alan Pakula's *Sophie's Choice*, a film about a woman who upon arriving at Auschwitz must choose which of her children will live. I then read the William Styron novel that the film was based on. My timing seems to have been about average. It

wasn't until the early 1980s that Hidden Children and Holocaust Survivor groups were started. It apparently took most of
us close to forty years to be able to begin to deal on a conscious
level with the horrors of our and our families' past.

My way of dealing with the horror was to dedicate myself
to taking whatever small steps were in my power to work
against war and other forms of violence. While I had in earlier
years been devastated by the unnecessary, senseless bloodshed
of the Vietnam War, and as early as 1964 had been a founding
member of the Ad Hoc Committee to End the War in Vietnam,
I did not at that time connect my intense horror at the war and
deep commitment to activism with my own and my family's
Holocaust experiences.

After I allowed myself to face my personal experience, my
efforts became conscious and focused. The result was my book,
*Boys Will Be Boys: Breaking the Link Between Masculinity
and Violence,* first published in 1991, and dedicated to the
memory of my family slaughtered in the Holocaust. There was
nothing unique about my reaction; as I started to research
books on violence, I soon realized that Holocaust survivors
were well represented among the authors.

In the late 1990s, I attended a meditation retreat with the
Vietnamese Buddhist monk Thich Nhat Hanh, and found out
that a group of Vietnam War veterans met every year at the
retreat. Thich Nhat Hanh had, in the early '90s, invited Vietnam veterans to join him, and the result was the formation of
what can best be described as an emotional support group. The
vets were generous in their "admission policy." As the author
of *Boys Will Be Boys* and as a Holocaust survivor, I became
part of the group.

The men, now in their fifties and sixties, were still cop-
ing emotionally with their war experiences. Those who killed
Vietnamese men, women, or children, or accidentally killed
comrades, tended to be in the most, often excruciating, pain.
The vets' horror at war matched mine and I felt very at home
with them. As I listened to them talk over and over again about

their eighteen-year-old naïveté — raised on John Wayne, war toys, and patriotism (some had volunteered to go and "defend democracy," others had not resisted the draft) — my admiration for my father's decision to go AWOL in the Russian–Polish War kept growing.

In these early years of the twenty-first century, a new generation of American soldiers is returning from yet another senseless, unnecessary war. Of the fortunate ones who did not lose their lives in Iraq or return amputees, blind, or otherwise physically disabled, about twenty percent suffer from post-traumatic stress disorder. This new tragedy (as well as the warfare that continues to plague so many other parts of the world) leads me to think often, and with intense sadness, of my father's letter to his granddaughter Nadia, expressing his hope that "peace will be in this crazy world" in her lifetime.

I can only applaud the thousands of soldiers who have gone and continue to go AWOL from the Iraqi war.

Had I not for so many years repressed the horror of my family history, I would have asked my parents many more questions when they were at an age to remember the particulars. Fortunately, my brother Joe, five years older than me, still has vivid memories of our exodus. I owe to him the description of how shortly after our departure from Brussels, we escaped bombings and drove through the burning town of Waregem. His stories about his experiences in Morocco have enriched that part of the book.

Because I didn't ask my parents, I had to create many of the details; this is particularly true of Part I, My Life in Poland. For example, my father's skeleton story about going AWOL consisted basically of the following: "I went to high school in Radomsk. I was supposed to finish, but they took me in the army. I was working in the kitchen peeling potatoes and onions all day. When they wanted to send me to the front, I ran away. They caught me on the frontier. I told them I was a student and so I was free from the army. They asked my high school if it was true and they said 'yes.'"

In Part III, World War II, my father's and mother's skeleton story about getting passports in Toulouse ran something like this: "We had to get Polish passports, so we went to the consulate, but when we got there French boy scouts were guarding the place. They told us that the consul had left for London, the consulate was closed, and we could not get passports. But we sneaked into the office and started to look in all the drawers; we found blank passports, and the official seal, so I filled everything out in Polish, stamped the passports, and we became Polish citizens again." This was sometimes followed by my father's story of the Polish consul in Brussels — "He threw us out because your mother started to laugh when he spoke Polish to her, and he was very insulted. This is why we didn't have Polish passports."

I offer these stories as examples of how my parents' stories form the foundation upon which the book is based, with my imagination as well as my research furnishing many of the details.

I tried to ground my narratives in my knowledge of my parents and their personalities. In the story of my father going AWOL, I have him meeting a pretty young girl on a train. The girl is a figment of my imagination, but my description of my father is accurate; he was indeed a very handsome and charming young man who did not "look Jewish," had a Polish surname, and spoke perfect Polish. The sadistic officer at the border is a figment of my imagination, but my father's handling of him is in keeping with the shrewdness he exhibited in later life.

In preparation for writing, I read some history including accounts of the Eastern front in World War I, the Russian–Polish War, and World War II in Belgium and France. I found films, books with pictures, and postcards from these periods.

Like so many Jews who emigrated to the U.S., immigrants from Przedborz formed a *Landsmannschaft* (a society of the natives of the same Polish town) at the turn of the twentieth century. In 1977, a Przedborz *Yizkor* book of remembrances was published. In it, a variety of people shared their memories of growing up in this small town, and in doing so provided me with a wealth of knowledge.

Thanks to the *Kielce-Radom Journal,* I found out more about the Polish province of Kielce in which my father grew up. In reading the Spring 2004 issue of this magazine, I learned that in October 1914, two Jews, Yaakov Hecherman and Shmuel Mose Astrian, were taken to the prison in the town of Kielce (located in the province of Kielce) and hung on charges of spying for the Germans. The article contains a detailed description of Astrian's dispute with a Gentile landowner that led to the landowner accusing him of spying for the Germans. After reading this, I surmised that since their home was not far from Kielce, my father, his brother, and their father were most likely taken to the same prison, and so I located the prison scenes in the book in Kielce. Kielce, by the way, became notorious after World War II when some of the local Gentiles killed the few Jewish natives that came back from concentration camps.

The depictions of family members killed in the Holocaust are based on my parents' descriptions. For example, my father always talked of his sister Balche as a very active, energetic person who loved to horse-ride around their farm and oversee the farmers who worked the land. My mother described her in the same way. My stories about her as a child are fictional, but based on these descriptions.

Balche did in real life marry and move to Czestochowa where her husband had a photography studio. They had a little girl and were killed in the Holocaust. There is no fiction here. Writing this book made my Polish family come alive for me as it never had before, which in turn led to my experiencing the horror of their deaths as I never had before. This was the most painful part of working on this book.

My father's sister Fella, with whom I contrast Balche, did in fact become blind for three months after her father's death. She came to live with my parents in Belgium in the early 1930s, and, together with my grandmother and Rifke, survived the

232 *He Walked through Walls*

war in Southern France. I knew Fella well. She was a very bright woman, a talented musician, and a hypochondriac. I cared for her a lot, and was saddened by the thwarted and depressed life she led.

I use these examples to give the reader some sense of how true stories and fictional details interact in the narrative.

At some point, while I was working on this book, my daughter Nadia asked, "How do you think *pépé* would feel about your writing his 'memoir'? Do you think it would bother him that you are writing in his voice?"

Until then, I had given only fleeting thought to these questions, for I had assumed that my father would be very pleased to have me try to recreate his voice and capture the experiences of war that led to his writing a letter to a three-month-old Nadia, telling her, "I hope that peace will be in this crazy world. All my life I have seen only wars. . . . I hope when you grow up you would not have terrible times like those your *pépé* went through."

I had assumed that my father would appreciate my recognizing and doing honor to his, and my mother's, extraordinary courage and survival skills; that he would want his story — and the story of the family he lost — to be told.

Answering my daughter's questions led me to formulate more clearly what I thought might be my father's reaction. Once again, I am putting words into his mouth. In response to some of the detailed narratives that I created around his stories, I hear him say, "The big stories are the way it happened, but you made up so many little stories around them. You put words in my mouth that I never said."

"I know that. But while you were alive, I never asked you exactly how it happened."

"It's a shame. You should have asked me."

"I know and I'm very sorry that I didn't."

"It would have been better if I had written down everything exactly like it happened."

"I agree, but you never did."

"I am a good storyteller, but I am not a writer. Tell me something. The people who read this, they will understand that the big stories are true, but not all the details, not all the little stories?"

"Yes, they will. I have made it very clear; I explain everything."

"So, in the end, I am glad you are telling the story."

Acknowledgments

M Y DEEPEST THANKS GO to my friend Judith Schiffer for her insightful and detailed critical comments, which undoubtedly improved the quality of the book. I am grateful to freelance editor Marlene Adelstein who read the very first version of the book; her comments led to an early restructuring of some parts of the manuscript. I also want to thank my friends Suzanne Goldberg and Kathryn Grody who read earlier versions for their comments and encouragement; I only wish I could extend my thanks to the late Barbara Harrison.

Thanks to Martin Rowe my editor at Lantern whose deep appreciation of the book confirmed my belief that my father's story would be of interest to people of radically different ethnic and religious backgrounds.

Thanks to my daughter Nadia Malinovich for taking time out of her very busy schedule to write the introduction to the book. Thanks to my brother Joe Mego for sharing his memories of our exodus.

My daughter Alisa Malinovich, my niece Debbie Mego, Chana Faszczak's granddaughter and her great-granddaughter Hélène Polak and Tania Lion-Polak, her niece and grandniece Bala and Joan Isaacs all helped in finding photos. My thanks go to them as well as to my young friend Jose Chicas and my son-in-law Max Silberztein for help in transferring photos into black and white.

When my father reminisced about his brothers and sisters, he would refer to "Moshe's wife and children" or "Balche's husband and little girl." I am grateful to Justyna Iwanicka whose help with research in Poland enabled me to obtain the first names of several family members. Thanks also to Justyna for the Polish, and to Renate Belville, Tania Lion-Polak and Janet Markovits for the German, Flemish, and Roumanian.

I am grateful to the Society Library in New York City and the New Paltz Public Library for providing great spaces with Internet access where I worked whenever I felt the need to get out of the house. Thanks to the librarians at the Center for Jewish History for facilitating my research.

And as always thanks to my husband Gary Ferdman whose love and encouragement are the underpinning of all my work.

About the Author

Myriam Miedzian holds a Ph.D. in philosophy from Columbia University and a Masters degree in Clinical Social Work from Hunter College. She has been a professor of philosophy at a number of universities, including Rutgers and the City University of New York. She is the author of two previous books, *Boys Will Be Boys* and *Generations,* and writes frequently on social, cultural, and political issues. Her articles, op-eds, and blogs have appeared in a variety of publications including *The Chicago Tribune, The Boston Globe, Social Research,* and *The Huffington Post.* Her TV appearances include The Oprah Winfrey Show, The Charlie Rose Show, and Larry King Live. She divides her time between New York City and New York's Hudson Valley. Website: *www.myriammiedzian.com*